About PICTURES

Terry Fenton

About PICTURES

Terry Fenton

edited by Allan Safarik

HAGIOS PRESS

Published by Hagios Press

Library and Archives Canada Cataloguing in Publication

Fenton, Terry, 1940-

About pictures / Terry Fenton.

Includes bibliographical references.

ISBN 978-0-9783440-9-2

1. Pictures--History. 2. Art--History. I. Title.

ND1143.F45 2009 760 C2009-902161-7

We wish to acknowledge all of the art galleries and agencies that provided images for use in this book.

Hagios Press gratefully acknowledges the support for the production of this book as provided by:

The Saskatchewan Arts Board

SINCE 1948 SASKATCHEWAN ARTS BOARD

The Canada Council for the Arts - Art Book Program

Canada Council for the Arts Conseil des Arts du Canada

The Cultural Industries Development Fund

Government of Saskatchewan

For more information on Hagios Press and our books: www.hagiospress.com

Printed and bound in Canada by Friesens Corporation

For Ken Noland

Painting is fortunate in requiring no more than a glance to attract and to fix.

—Eugene Delacroix, journal entry, Sept. 1, 1859

Table of Contents

Acknowledgements

First of all, thanks to Allan Safarik, who sorted through my web site and found the germ of a book. The book that follows is more focused, but it wouldn't have been done without his strong push and encouragement. Thanks, as well, to Paul Wilson and Hagios Press for undertaking to publish another art book. That shows courage and, I hope, foresight from a small publisher in the Canadian West.

A large part of the publication of art books has to do with acquiring images and permissions. Many artists and museums have contributed to this, some of them freely. Thanks to all, but especially to the Victoria and Albert Museum, the Mendel Art Gallery, and the J. Paul Getty Museum, for their generosity. The Boston Museum of Fine Arts, The Museum of Modern Art, The National Gallery in London, and the Frick Museum made fine photographs or great paintings available. Contemporary artists were helpful and supportive whenever contacted. The estates of Jules Olitski and Morris Louis, the Adolph and Esther Gottlieb Foundation, Kenneth Noland, Douglas Haynes, Robert Christie, Orest Semchishen, and James Walsh were helpful and gave permissions freely. I only wish that I could have included more artists whose work I admire.

Finally, I must thank my wife, Sheila, for putting up with me while I wrote and for providing many helpful correctives.

Foreword

This book is meant to be an introduction to the nature, development, types, media, and appreciation of what we call "pictures." I've written it for the general reader and art lover. It's more commonplace book than history. I use the word "picture" in a restricted sense because it strikes me that the picture, as we understand it today, fits within that conception. My account of its development is sketchy to say the least and admits of many exceptions and enlargements. By and large I've concentrated on the obvious because what's taken for granted is often misunderstood or misconstrued or simply missed—like the purloined letter. I hasten to add that I'm not an art historian, a fact that will be obvious to those who are.

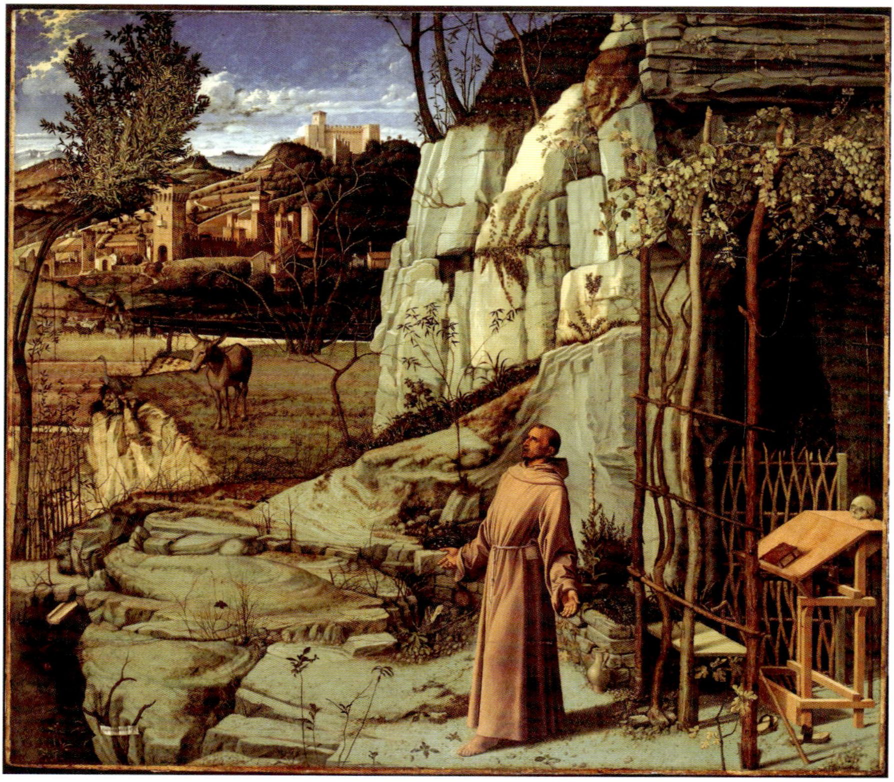

Giovanni Bellini (Italian c. 1430 - 1516) *St. Francis in the Desert*, 1480.
Oil and tempera on poplar panel,
49 in. x 55 7/8 in. The Frick Museum, Henry Clay Frick Bequest.
Photograph © The Frick Collection, New York

This book is about pictures

St. Francis in the Desert is my favorite painting. The great Venetian painter, Giovanni Bellini, painted it in the late 15th Century, when oil paint was new to Italy. It's painted on a wooden panel (before canvas became *de rigeur*) over an underpainting in tempera. In the Flemish manner, oil paint was added in thin washes over the tempera to give warmth and depth to the colour. The *St. Francis* is a rectangular picture as well. The shape seems commonplace to our eyes, but was on the way to becoming the picture format that stretched canvas and the easel picture nailed down for centuries to come.

The subject itself is wonderfully appropriate to my theme. *St. Francis in the Desert*? Perhaps; but to my eyes the desert looks pretty juicy. The painting strikes me rather as an accompaniment to St. Francis's *Canticle of Brother Sun* in which the Saint praises God's Creation. In the painting, the Saint greets the new day and the visible splendor of His world. In a sense he becomes an emblem of the painter, who takes the whole visible world for his subject—not just a figure or figures, but sheer visibility itself.

The landscape in this painting isn't just a stage or setting: it's an active participant in the whole. It completes the painting as a picture, in a sense foreshadowing landscape painting, that subject without a subject which came to play such an important role in Western pictorial art.

EYESIGHT

As pictures are a form of visual art, and as the visual arts address the eyes, it's worth taking a look at how eyes work. It might offer a clue to the nature of pictures.

A common way of explaining how the eye works has been to compare it to a camera. Like a camera, the eye uses a lens to transfer information to a screen (the retina), which is "developed" by the brain.

But does the eye see in "pictures?"

The eye doesn't capture still images. In this it's more like a video camera. (According to Oliver Sacks, our perception of the moving visual field may consist of a rapid progression of "stills" like a movie.)[1] Nevertheless, the mental impression is that of a continuously changing visual field.

The retina isn't a flat rectangular screen. While its lack of flatness may not be significant, its lack of rectangularity certainly is. The retina is divided into rods and cones, which respond to light in different ways. Colour-sensitive cones occupy the centre of the retina, which divides eyesight roughly into focused and peripheral vision. A small central area of the retina called the fovea has high visual acuity. The fovea is more or less circular, has a concentration of cones, and covers about two degrees of the visual field. There's no clear boundary between the fovea and the periphery. In other words, our eyes don't see in terms of delimited pictures equal in focus from centre to sides.

Our eyes are constantly moving so that the brain is continually stitching together material provided by the fovea and periphery. This enormously expands our sense of the visual field.

The eye perceives colour in low light differently from film and digital cameras. This may have something to do with rods and cones, but more, I suspect, with the way the brain filters colour. Camera images have a strong blue shift in low light that isn't present in eyesight. Added to this is the fact that we see in a more "close-valued" way than cameras do: we see more colour in shadows and dim light.

Nevertheless our conception of eyesight continues to be explained by the metaphor of the camera and the photograph, just as our conception of brain activity is likened to the computer. The analogy in either case isn't perfect. Brains don't just compute; eyes don't see in pictures.

WHY PICTURES?

Nowadays pictures are omnipresent, so much so that we presume they've been with us always. Not so—not even in Western culture and not in many other parts of the world until the last century.

When I went to art school in the late 1950s, my fellow students and I scorned works of art that were merely "pictures." In our minds the word suggested cheap and commercial things: photographs in magazines, commercial still lifes of flowers and the like; everything but "fine art." Fine art was "painting." The fact that the fine art we admired was found primarily in art publications and colour slides didn't sink in. We knew what it was before we'd seen much of the real thing.

My ideas have changed, mainly through increased exposure to art in galleries and museums as well as artists' studios. I've come to see that most works in the Western fine art tradition, at least since the late Middle Ages, were *pictures* made with paint. In confirmation I cite Henri Matisse, who referred to his own paintings as "pictures." If the word was good enough for him, it's good enough for me.

A stimulus to my changed point of view came with the rise of Minimal and Conceptual Art in the 1960s. Painting in that decade became stripped down and emptied out. Many began to proclaim it dying or dead. Benumbed objects and arrangements occupied space in museums and galleries and seemed, as I myself once had, to regard mere pictures with contempt. Amidst this, I discovered that some artists painted abstract pictures that were freshly pictorial and brimmed with life. When that happened I realized I'd passed over to the other side.

Since that time my experience of art, both past and present, suggests that much of what we call the fine art of painting has been governed by picture making, and that the picture is a priceless construct of a few high civilizations. For a variety of reasons I'll focus on our own.

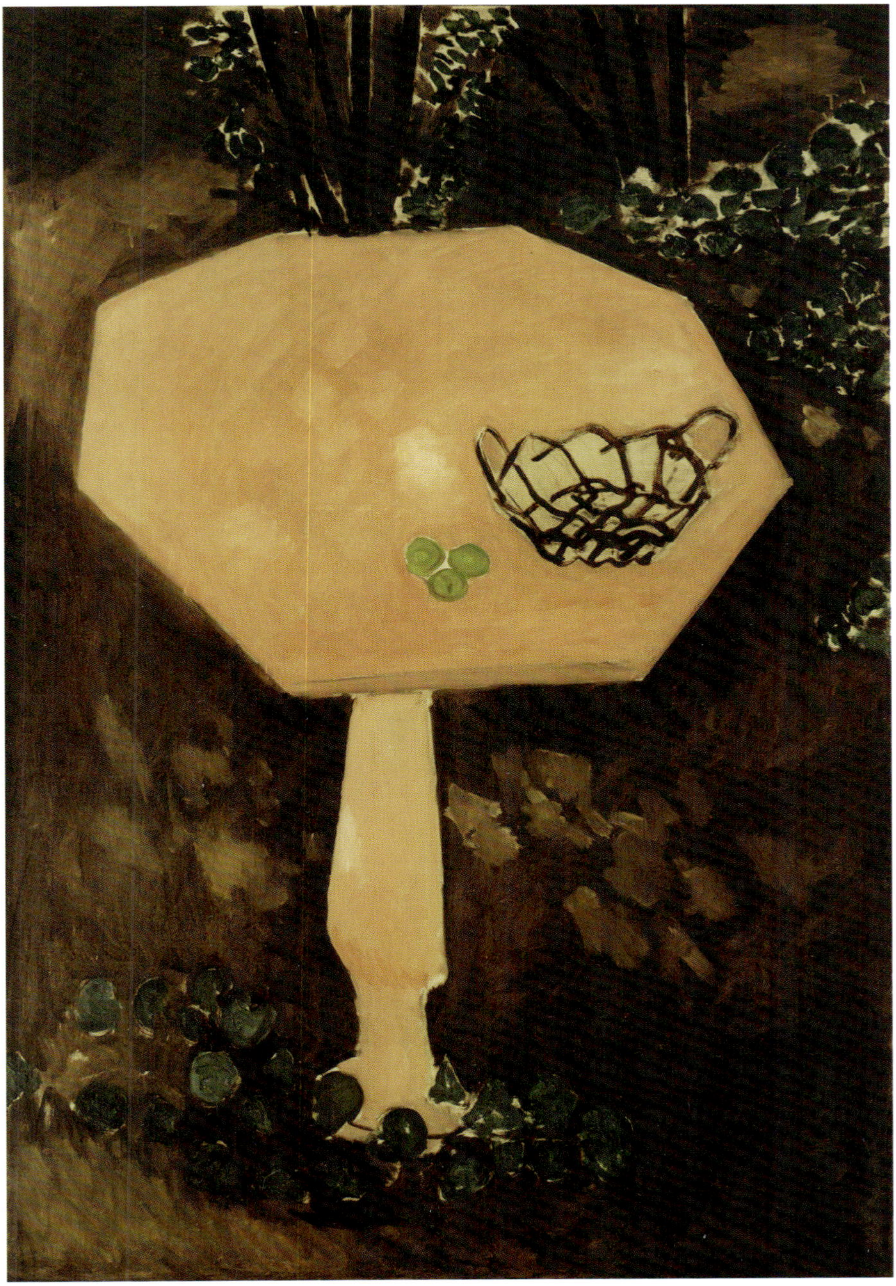

Henri Matisse, (French 1869-1954) *The Rose Marble Table*, 1917. Issy-les-Molineaux, spring-summer, 1917. Oil on canvas, 57 ½ x 38 ¼ in. The Museum of Modern Art, New York, Mrs. Simon Guggenheim Fund.
© Succession H. Matisse, Paris / ARS, NY
Digital Image © The Museum of Modern Art,/Licensed by SCALA / Art Resource, NY

SOME QUESTIONS

> Expression, for me, does not reside in passions glowing in a human face or manifested by violent movement. The entire arrangement of my picture is expressive: the place occupied by the figures, the empty spaces around them, the proportions, everything has its share.... In a picture every part will be visible and will play its appointed role, whether it be principal or secondary.... A work of art must be harmonious in its entirety.[2]
>
> —Henri Matisse

What is a picture?

To begin with, it's not something fixed and final: pictures, and the conventions that inhabit them, have changed over centuries and will continue to change.

Generally speaking, a picture is an arrangement of visual elements on or within a delimited surface. That said, pictures are more than just flat objects, just as books are more than bundles of paper. When we look at pictures we see coherent arrangements, ones that create the illusion of some kind of space within a surface and defined shape. Above all, pictures are *illusions*.

Over several centuries we've learned to see these illusions as pictures because, by looking, we've learned many of the conventions that inhabit them. People who haven't experienced these conventions can't "understand" some kinds of pictures, black and white photographs for example. On the other hand, I suspect that photographic reproductions have conditioned us to see some works as pictures that weren't originally seen that way.

Why are most picture rectangles?

Probably because most walls and pages are.

The wheel has been called the greatest human invention, but variations of the rectangle should get equal billing. The rectangle is the simplest, most reduced geometric figure.

Rectangles fit together neatly to make larger rectangles. They're inherently vertical and horizontal. They're the foundations of civilized architecture. By and large they're the format of the walls we live within and the pages of books.

A picture rectangle is a neutral and stable shape. It doesn't call attention to itself in relation to walls and floors and pages. As a result, it helps to isolate the picture from its surroundings and guarantees that its enclosing shape won't overpower its internal configuration.

Are pictures necessarily works of art?

Necessarily yes, even if the art isn't very good. But just because a thing is a work of art doesn't mean that it can be experienced aesthetically by anyone. That's the catch.

Some pictures aren't intended to be works of art. Some are meant simply to be illustrations, to show or to explain in a way that words can't. This is true especially of many photographs and drawings. That's the most common meaning of the phrase, "a picture is worth a thousand words."

How important are picture titles?

They're as important as they *appear*.

In the past, many pictures went untitled and titles were added by later generations, often by scholars in the 19th and 20th Centuries. These titles continue to change, subject to discoveries of iconography as well as academic fashion. Abstract artists have often provided titles that suggest something of the evocation their pictures possess or simply as a means of identification. As with music, so it is with pictures: titles don't always explain, though they often hint and allude.

Is there a right way or a wrong way to look at a picture?

There's no secret method, apart from keeping your eyes open and keeping an open mind. The first is easy. The second isn't.

Certain conventions let us know that what we're seeing is a picture, just as certain relations of sound let us know that we're hearing music instead of noise. But sometimes conventions can get in the way of appreciation, especially when they lead us to expect something that isn't there nor need be, a problem some people have with abstraction.

Sometimes, people mistake recognition for appreciation. They *think* they like certain pictures because they've seen reproductions of them or pictures like them, or they recognize the subject matter.

Trust your eyes. Trust your instincts. Don't analyze. Let the picture come to you.

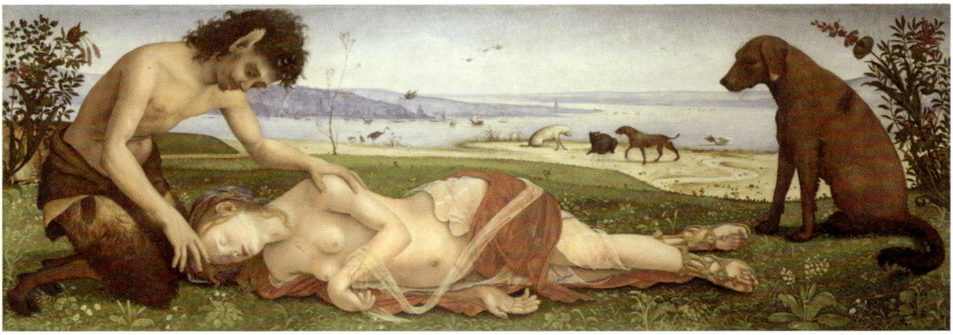

Piero di Cosimo (Italian 1462-1522), *A Satyr mourning over a Nymph*, 1495. Oil on panel, 25 ¾ x 72 ½ in. The National Gallery, London. Photograph © The National Gallery, London.

In representational art, subject matter is often elusive. This masterpiece by Piero di Cosimo is a case in point, especially because subject matter plays such an important role in the expression of the picture. There've been attempts to find the subject in mythology, especially in Ovid's *Metamorphoses*, but none have been convincing. The National Galley identifies it as *A Satyr Mourning Over a Nymph*, which accounts for two of the figures. But what role does the dog play? After all, it's one of the three major figures. And what about all the creatures cavorting in the background? The fact that the three main figures consist of human, half-human half-animal, and animal must be significant. In this case, knowing the literary meaning, even if discovered, would do little to affect the picture's sympathetic power. It's one of the tenderest pictures in Western art.

Should you look at all pictures the same way, whether they're abstract paintings, representational paintings or photographs?

Yes, despite all arguments to the contrary (which often begin, "But everyone knows..." or "Surely you don't mean to suggest..." or "What you fail to recognize...")

Just look. Let the picture teach you its language.

What is a painting?

A picture made with paint. Other ways of making pictures include drawing, printmaking, and photography.

In our culture most paintings are intended to be works of art, whereas many drawings, prints, and photographs aren't.

What is a representational picture?

Between about 1400 and 1900 pictures were thought of primarily as spaces, like empty stages, which could be filled with representations of objects drawn from the visible world. The camera was invented because of the precedent set by representational painting.

"Representation" is a more accurate way of saying "realism" (since both abstract and representational pictures are "real" objects).

Representational art attempts, in one way or another, to create an illusion of the visible world. Theoretically that's how it differs from abstraction. In reality there's no hard and fast dividing line between the two. Abstraction and representation are just descriptive terms. They have nothing whatever to do with whether art is good or less than good.

What is a photograph?

Photography was a 19th Century invention. It used a camera, a picture-making machine, to record images photo-chemically.

Not every photographic image is a picture in any meaningful sense. Some are simply copies—of a printed page, for example, or an x-ray—but most are pictures.

Are painted pictures better than photographs?

A medium in itself can't guarantee aesthetic success. Against a vapid painting can be placed a successful photograph. Photographs by Eugene Atget, Lewis Hine, Walker Evans and many others are more than mere records of fact. They assemble those raw facts into coherent works of art, what might be called pictorial stories. Their pictures reward attention like good paintings do, but do it differently.

What is an abstract picture?

Basically, it's one that doesn't try to represent the visible world. (This doesn't mean that it represents something else.)

Abstract painters use flat patterns, geometric motifs, emphatic textures, and intense colours—the elements of traditional decorative art—to make pictures. Some of these devices are "abstracted" from the visible world; others have been invented or imagined. Everything in abstract art is affected in some way by visual experience, but it's often impossible to say or show how.

What is modern painting?

In the late 19th Century, some artists began to think that the material characteristics of painting itself, the fact that paintings were flat rectangular surfaces covered with paint, had more to do with whether paintings were good or bad than the fact that they represented things or told stories. As a result, artists concentrated more and more on these "abstract" properties of painting and gradually abandoned representations of the visible world.

This process is sometimes called Modernism. The painting, which resulted from it, is called modernist or modern painting. Modernism isn't good in itself. In the hands of some artists it produced masterpieces; in the hands of many it led to pictures that were incoherent or dull.

Is some modern art a hoax?

Hans Christian Andersen's story about *The Emperor's New Clothes* seems to apply to the public's inability to appreciate modern art. Because traditional conventions and techniques were abandoned in many 20th Century paintings, and because so much depended on the viewer's willingness to appreciate the new, many people suspected that modern art was itself a hoax or that it had been taken over by charlatans. Certainly, some modern pictures are as dismally empty as the emperor was naked and some people lavish praise on the worst of them, but generally speaking, the artists who painted them seriously meant to make "art."

Ironically, really good art often causes more suspicion than mediocre "art." Because it modifies and discards conventions, it seems to lack the meanings that had accompanied them. Moreover, when new art is good it sometimes demands attention in a puzzling way. Irritation sometimes precedes aesthetic reward.

Why do some adults enjoy abstract paintings by young children but dislike abstract paintings by adults?

I suspect they like the idea of children's art better than the art itself.

In fact some people seem to like the idea of art better than individual works of art. They tend to be artistic do-gooders rather than picture-lovers.

What do pictures mean?

The question might be rephrased as "how do pictures mean?" Whatever meaning pictures have is a kind of visual, not verbal, meaning.

STEPS TO PICTURES

Familiar as they now are, pictures weren't common to all cultures and periods. They've been with us in the Western World since the late Middle Ages. They're ubiquitous in the form of rectangular paintings, prints, and more recently photographs. So familiar have they become that we've all but forgotten their unique character. For the picture is an artificial construct, like written literature or musical composition. So I'll speak of the category as "the picture" as one speaks of "the symphony" or "the novel."

The picture grew up hand in hand with aesthetic value: perhaps not as completely as did music, but more emphatically than writing. Writing, of course, is a large and loose category. Its aesthetic aspect is largely confined to literature—to poetry and prose fiction. At the other extreme, music seems inseparable from aesthetic value; that's its main purpose. Even musical signals—bugle calls and the like—are memorable because of an aesthetic connotation.

It might be argued that the picture sought to bring the sequential images of the frieze into something more immediate and self-contained. For the picture has a quality that the sequential art forms can't rival, the quality of immediacy. As Delacroix suggested, no matter how complex it may be, a picture asks to be taken in "at a glance." When it can't be for one reason or another, its power is diminished.

On the surface, this immediacy appears to be a limitation. But is it? A seeming escape is the motion picture. But in its transcendence of immediacy the motion picture drains the picture of its unique aesthetic character, nudging it into the realm of literature and theatre.

Prehistoric Painting

One of the chief characteristics of man is uprightness: man stands erect and faces forward with binocular vision. Why, if binocular vision enables one to see objects in three dimensions, do we take such interest in flat surfaces more or less parallel to our faces? But that so-called pleasure must be qualified: we enjoy these surfaces when they're broken up in some way, most commonly with characters or images. Prehistoric examples of this have been found on the walls of caves.

Why caves? I presume that the simplest answer might be that the paintings on their walls have survived. Caves presented surfaces that were unencumbered with vegetation and debris, and not subject to weathering. Because paint is notoriously fragile, prehistoric paintings on other surfaces have long since deteriorated.

Cave paintings aren't "pictures" in the sense that we understand the word today. The paintings tended to be unique figures of animals and animal groups, painted with considerable vitality. When more than one figure was involved, the relation was causal or accidental rather than pictorial. There was no "framing," no completion outside the individual figure or group.

One sees something of the same thing in Inuit prints from the Canadian North, though some Western pictorial conventions have been imposed, if only in the form of rectangular sheets of paper suitable for framing.

Prehistoric representational painting can be seen as a preliminary step towards more structured image making as well as writing. One can only wonder at the character of early speech. That it coexisted with speech can hardly be doubted; speech must have preceded it. But here, in early visual communication, is the germ of the universal language of visual art.

Friezes and Figures

I suspect that the horizontal line on an upright surface became one of the first prerequisites of visual art. The arrangement of images that we take so much for granted in civilized life wasn't omnipresent in the past. It was hard won.

Agriculture and settlement had produced permanent buildings. These in turn led to the tendency to rectangularity and to flat vertical walls, a consequence of brick building and post and lintel structure. Walls were often decorated with friezes of one kind or another.

These horizontal arrangements of figures didn't appear at first against a horizon: that didn't come until fairly recently. The horizontal line when it first appeared was an abstraction of the ground, of the level surface that man walks upon. The frieze arranged figures along that horizontal ground plane. It seems to have been the first type of civilized image organization.

The frieze might be called a "sequential image format" rather than a true picture. There are many kinds of friezes, some purely decorative, some in *bas relief*, but I'm here

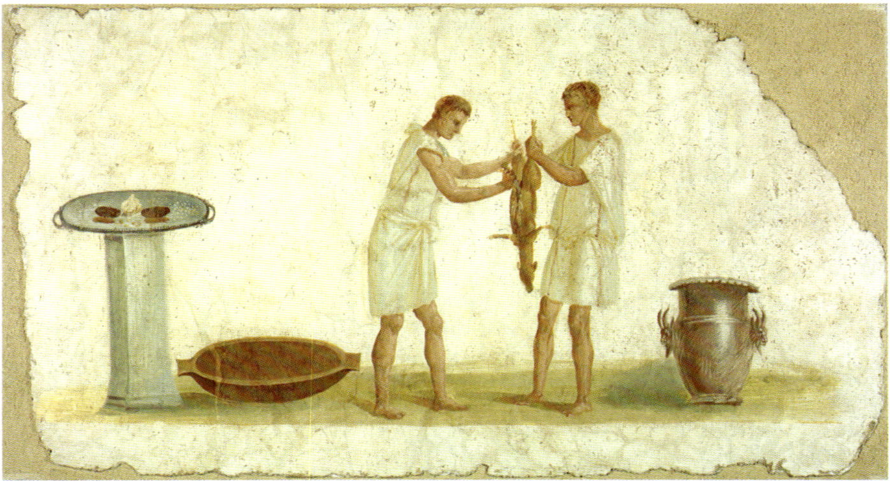

Unknown Roman, Italy, A.D. 50 – 75. *Wall Fragment with a Scene of Meal Preparation.* Plaster and pigment 27 3/8 x 50 x 1 3/8 in. The J. Paul Getty Museum. Photograph © 2009, the J. Paul Getty Trust

concerned with the frieze as an early form of painting that was common up to and including the Roman and Byzantine era.

The primary aesthetic unit in the frieze was the figure or figure group. Many friezes could be "read" sequentially; they could suggest a succession of events or a procession, something that more recent pictures can't easily accomplish.

But the frieze could also be truncated into a narrow compartment. There it could contain a single figure or figure group, sometimes within a rectangular border. The important thing to remember about friezes or compartmented images was that the bottom edge was primary, insofar as it anchored the ground, that sides were secondary and that the top was something of an afterthought. This became increasingly apparent in the late Middle Ages, when the tops of these contained images sometimes became elaborately architectural, terminating in arches or triangular peaks.

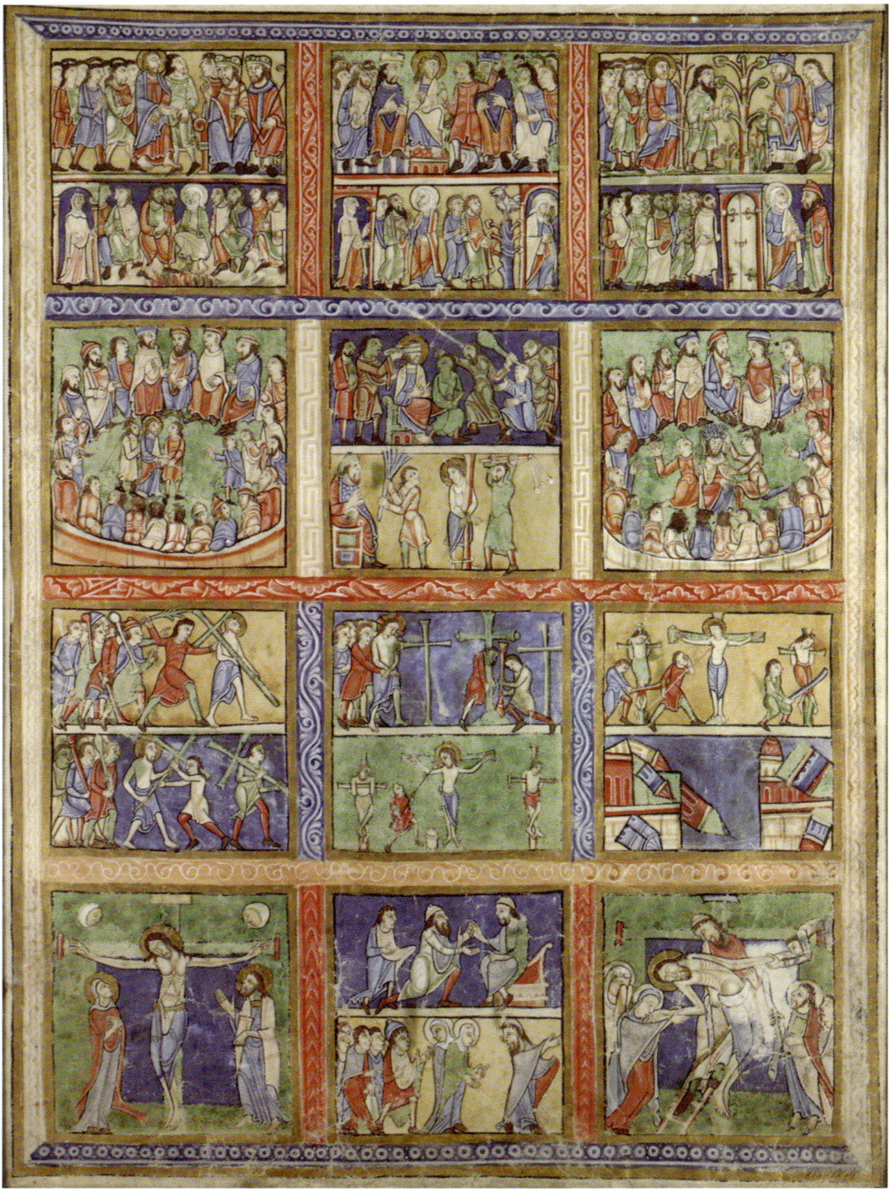

Canterbury, England. Leaf from a Psalter (Eadwine Psalter) with scenes from the New Testament, ca. 1155-1160. Watercolour with egg or gum binding medium on vellum, 15 ½ x 11 ½ in. Victoria and Albert Museum.
Photograph © Victoria and Albert Museum, London

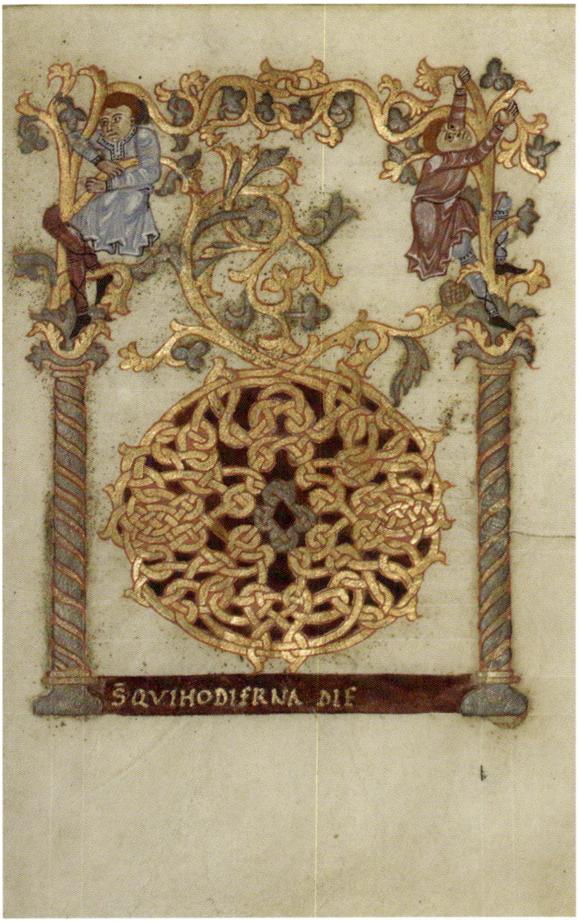

Two illuminated pages from manuscripts. They give some idea of the range of invention that can be found in this extraordinary art form. The leaf from the *Eadwine Psalter* shows a series of events from the Gospels within borders, comic book fashion. The contained scenes are painted like tiny friezes upon a continuous ground plane. Backgrounds are blank.

The *Decorated Initial D* in the second reproduction is hardly a picture at all although the gilded initial is "inhabited" by two figures and rests upon columns that share a ground plane.

When the printed book emerged in the mid 15th Century, connoisseurs maintained that it wouldn't last because it was cheap and ugly. It was indeed cheaper than the manuscript, though not necessarily ugly. The printed book had merits of its own and illumination, in any event, was unable to compete with the framed and self-contained panel picture that emerged in the 14th Century.

MS. Attributed to Nivardus Of Milan Ottonian, Fleury, France. *Decorated Initial D.* about 1000 - 1025. Tempera colours, gold, and silver on parchment 9 ⅛ x 7 ¹⁄₁₆ in. The J. Paul Getty Museum. Photograph© 2009, the J. Paul Getty Trust

Manuscript Illumination

The primary pictorial art in Europe from roughly AD 600 to 1200 was manuscript illumination. The great majority of manuscripts were in the codex format, a bound book with parchment pages made from thinly scraped animal skins, which replaced the papyrus scroll in the late Roman period. The codex was the prototype for the book as we know it today.

The book arose in the great interregnum of European history, the so-called Dark Ages, replete with barbarian invasions and Christian monasticism. In fact, before AD 1000 virtually all manuscript production came from scriptoria in monasteries. (Later on some of the work was shopped out.) Most of the books illuminated were religious works, many of extraordinary beauty.

Illuminations were book illustrations. They always served and enhanced the text. The primary aesthetic unit was always the page. But the very fact that the page was rectangular may have reinforced a tendency to conceive images within its parameters.

Until the 15th century, illuminations were at best quasi-pictorial. Many were purely decorative—pattern pages, decorated and inhabited initials and borders. In many manuscripts, illustrations and decorations were intertwined. Some of the illustrations can be seen as pictures as we understand them today, but usually in a rudimentary sense. Until about 1350, figures stood in a kind of shallow relief upon a ground plane parallel to the bottom of the picture, much as they had in the frieze. In effect, the contained "pictures" in manuscripts were something like squeezed friezes: the bottom edge was paramount, synonymous with the ground, the sides were secondary, the top was often a decorative addition.

Illumination certainly anticipated the panel painting that emerged in the 14th Century, but by that time panel paintings had the advantage of picture frames, albeit anticipated and influenced by the borders and architectural surrounds in many illuminations. The great age of illumination began to decline in the 14th Century when illusionistic pictures began to break the flatness of the page and the print. To my eyes, the fully pictorial illuminations of 14th and especially 15th Century manuscripts seldom compete with panel painting.

Consolidation of the Picture

Several things happened between 1300 and 1450 to consolidate the new era of picture making.

1. Paper was introduced into Europe. It was cheaper and more abundant than parchment, which it gradually replaced in book production. By the 15th Century, its

low cost made sketching materials available for artists (they'd previously relied on pattern books and expensive parchment.) Thus began the great age of drawing and sketching from life.

2. A growing middle class created a demand for portable panel paintings. The rectangular picture format began to emerge in these and in the predellas (bottom portions) of altarpieces.

3. The growing interest in naturalism led to attempts to reproduce the natural world more faithfully. In terms of picture-making this resulted in:

   - The discovery of the horizon
   - The discovery of linear perspective
   - The discovery of aerial perspective

4. The invention of oil paint

After this, the transition from panel to canvas in late 15th Century Venice confirmed the rectangle as the primary format for oil painting. In addition to ease of preparation, the rectangle had the advantage of simple and neutral containment.

MATERIALS / MEDIA

MEDIUM

"Medium: that by or through which anything is accomplished, conveyed, or carried on."

—The Living Webster Encyclopedic Dictionary.

"For each art has its own medium and that medium is especially fitted for one kind of communication. Each medium says something that cannot be uttered as well or as completely in any other tongue."

—John Dewey, *Art As Experience*.

The medium of painting is a complex of materials and conventions, ones that have been modified and augmented over the years. Its materials tend to be various paints and the surfaces that receive and support them. Its conventions involve the use of those materials. Some conventions support representation and figuration; others don't.

The medium of painting (like many other media) has often been compared to a language. Like language, it communicates through symbols, usages, and inflections. Unlike language, it also communicates through material and optical presence.

The medium of painting isn't fixed and final. It changes, albeit slowly. This development is brought about by changes in materials and in the conventions that govern their use. These don't necessarily coincide. Thus, the medium can't be considered apart from its history.

As I've suggested above, the medium of painting isn't the only means of making pictures. Various printmaking media are closely related. Photography is more distinctly separate.

Materials

Materials enable rather than dictate. Their influence is subtle. Often they don't create new conventions so much as they reinforce some existing ones and, in so doing, lead to the abandonment of others. Above all, materials tend to be agents of stability and continuity. For example, oil paint dominated pictorial art until the emergence of photography in the 19th Century, and continued to dominate painting until the 1950s. In some ways its domination remains, as many of its characteristics have been built into the acrylic paints that have all but replaced oils for fine art. The capacity of materials to resist change is also exemplified by photography's bias towards representation. The medium has resisted abstraction for well over a century, despite the efforts of some photographers.

Paint

Paint is the material that gives painting its name. It provides colour and covers surfaces.

Most paints consist of coloured powders (pigments) suspended in a colourless, glue-like binder.

Fresco

Pigment mixed with water is applied on a thin layer of wet, fresh, lime mortar or plaster. The wet plaster absorbs the pigment, so a binder is not required. When the plaster dries it reacts with the air and this chemical reaction fixes the pigment in the plaster.

Fresco is used primarily for painting directly on walls. It was used in antiquity and throughout the Middle Ages and Renaissance.

Because of its expanse, wall painting favors arrangements of figure groups rather than pictures *per se*. Michelangelo's great frescos in the Sistine Chapel are dominated by inspired figures and figure groups. At best they're quasi-pictorial.

Egg tempera

Powdered pigments hand-ground into fresh egg yolk produce a permanent paint that dries quickly. The paint has clear bright colours and, because of its quick drying time, must be applied thinly in short, hatched strokes. Used in manuscript illumination, it was carried into panel paintings by the Italian masters of the 14th and 15th Centuries prior to the introduction of oil paint. The great 15th Century Flemish oil painters used it for underpainting.

Oil paint

> ... I make the positive statement to you, that oil painting is the Art of arts, that it is sculpture, drawing, and music all in one... There is no other human skill so great or so wonderful...[3]
>
> — John Ruskin

The use of oil painting is recorded as early as the 12th Century in Northern Europe. But in the early 15th Century the virtuoso handling of the medium on panel by Flemish painters such as Jan van Eyck and Rogier van der Weyden led to its spread throughout Europe.

In the hands of the early Flemish painters, oil paint was used to glaze in thin translucent layers over an underpainting in tempera. Their paint was probably thinned with stand oil, which was stickier than linseed oil and adhered to the surface without drying quickly. Glazes added depth to colour and allowed blending and blurring, which enabled artists to model subjects with greater proficiency and to bathe them and their surroundings in an illusion of light and atmosphere. Giovanni Bellini in Venice most likely acquired the technique from Antonello da Messina, who'd picked it up in Flanders. As I've mentioned above, Bellini painted his *St. Francis* in the Flemish manner.

After Bellini, the great Venetian painters—Giorgione, Titian, Tintoretto, and Veronese—virtually invented a new medium when they found a way to apply thickened oil paint to stretched canvas. This nailed down the format of the easel picture for centuries to come. In their hands, oil paint became a highly flexible medium, one that admitted application in both thick impasto and fine detail. Brushstrokes themselves became descriptive and expressive. These properties made it especially suitable to suggest the character of different surfaces, from polished marble to dazzling jewels, from soft velvet to luminous highlights on polished metal or glass. In doing so, they established the painterly (*malerish*) foundations of painting or, as Delacroix was to put it, perfected painting's "material means." It also brought a new richness and expressive power to colour.

Colour

Colour is one of the keys to the success of painting as a pictorial art, if only because it maneuvers what might normally be decoration into a more complex and evocative unity. The history of colour in Western painting is a study in itself. In the mid 19th Century Manet and the French Impressionists gave it new life. Neo-Impressionists like Van Gogh and Gauguin enhanced its expressive potential, while Cézanne reinforced its structural power. In the 20th Century Henri Matisse used colour with a new independence. By the 1950s, American painters like Mark Rothko, Adolf Gottlieb, Barnett Newman, Morris Louis, and Kenneth Noland used colour as a primary means of structure and expression in large abstract paintings.

Paper

Painting based on direct observation of the visible world and not on preconceptions or conventional images of it emerged with enormous impact in the second and third decades of 15th Century. Painting after nature—the representation of landscape based upon direct observation—emerged concurrently.

Naturalism of this high order had been long in preparation, stimulated by both late medieval manuscript illumination and Gothic sculpture: in a sense, painters strove to emulate the naturalistic figures of sculpture with the luminous colour of illumination. This wasn't accomplished easily. The conventions, which dominated painting at the time, resisted their impulse, favoring schematic figures and flat, blank backgrounds. Until the van Eycks, painters lacked the genius to accomplish their ambitions. Yet even the van Eycks' genius may have been insufficient apart from new means. Conveniently, these were provided by two great technological developments of the early 15th Century, oil paint and manufactured paper.

Of the two, paper may well have been the more important. Although it had long been known in the Oriental and Muslim worlds it hadn't become widely available in Europe until the early 14th Century, at which time industrial production made it cheaper than parchment. Paper quickly made itself indispensable, both practically and creatively. Its most revolutionary consequence was the printed book. But its importance went far beyond that. Its light weight and low cost meant that it was disposable, something the West appears to have uniquely seized upon. It quickly became the standard material for record keeping, correspondence, and financial transactions. In the visual arts, paper's disposability was no less consequential. There it gave new scope to drawing, making possible a great variety of preparatory studies for paintings.

Before the arrival of paper, artists were severely limited in their ability to replicate nature. How to train one's hand to capture appearances in the absence of a cheap, disposable material to practice upon? Paper enabled the eye to teach the hand in a new

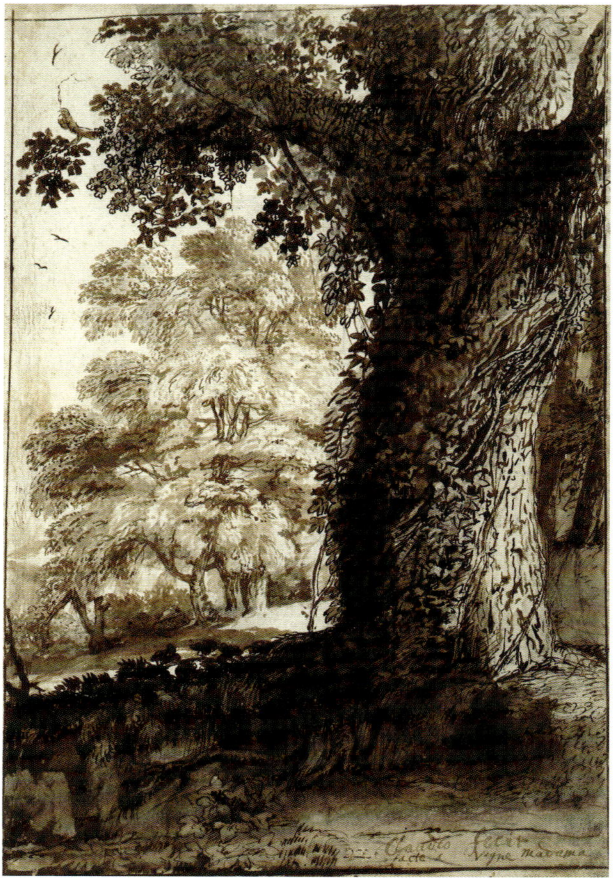

Claude Lorrain (French, worked in Italy 1600-1682), *Study of an Oak Tree.* Ink and wash on paper, 13 x 8 ⅞ in. The British Museum. Photograph © The Trustees of the British Museum

way, and artists were quick to take advantage of it. By the 16th Century, they'd taken to drawing from life prodigiously and for a variety of purposes, from anatomical studies to rapid layout sketches for painted pictures. The great era of old master drawings had begun.

The painted landscape, as we know it today was inconceivable apart from the portable and disposable support provided by paper. As a result, between the 15th and 18th Centuries, the drawn sketch on paper became the primary means by which artists recorded nature directly.

The van Eycks created space around and behind their figures and gave them air to breathe. This space and air came from their invention of aerial perspective, which exploited oil paint, the other great emergent art technology of 15th Century. Because of its range of colour and ability to blend and blur, oil paint could suggest the illusion of distance through gradations of colour and tone.

It was only a matter of time before the illusionistic backgrounds of oil paintings took on a life of their own and became themselves the picture subject. This came about gradually through the diminution of figures in relation to the whole. Such transitional paintings suggested that figures were harmonious parts of the natural world. Eventually they could be abandoned altogether.

These "pure" landscape paintings from the 17th and 18th Centuries reinforced the concept of the picture as an aesthetic object, a work of art to be appreciated in and of itself, rather than a means tell a story or make a point. The viewer responded intuitively and aesthetically to the painted landscape as he might to a real scene. This tendency to capture landscape as a vehicle of feeling is suggested in the 17th Century by what Roger Fry called Claude Lorraine's "golden glow" as well as by the dramatic skies of Dutch painters like Ruisdael. When the sky became a major participant in the depicted landscape, disinterested appreciation of the picture became a primary artistic objective.

However, painting after nature didn't mean painting on site; until the late 18th Century it meant *drawing* on site. Although artists after the 15th Century and later worked from nature with pencil or ink, the problem of working with colour eluded them. In the early 16th Century, Albrecht Dürer, to be sure, had painted small watercolours on his travels, but his innovation remained undeveloped for two and a half centuries.

In the 15th through 17th Centuries, painting in oils was confined to the studio, where models, draperies, and props could be arranged to the artist's satisfaction. To paint in colours directly from nature called for a host of other enabling factors, particularly improved means of travel and the availability of lightweight equipment and materials. In the 17th century Claude Lorraine worked from nature in ink and wash. While his works in this medium have a "modern" directness, his studio paintings seem conventional in comparison.

A major step forward came in the 18th Century, when British artists like Alexander Cozens and his son John Robert used watercolour to capture nature directly. Their subjects were drawn from the Grand Tour as well as rural England. To them we owe our sympathetic perception of alpine scenery. Because it brought painting with colour out of doors, watercolour became preeminently a landscape medium. It was developed by some great English painters of the late 18th and early 19th Centuries: Thomas Girtin, J. M. W. Turner, and John Sell Cotman among others. John Constable enlarged the tradition yet again by painting sketches from directly nature in oils (often on paper,) enabling a more direct connection between the sketch and the studio picture. In this he anticipated and influenced the great main stream of 19th Century painting.

Canvas

Canvas came into its own in 16th Century Venice as a ground upon which to apply oil paint.

Before that time, oil painting had been done primarily on wooden panels. However, in the damp climate of Venice, wood panels tended to deteriorate. The solution was to paint on canvas, a light, flexible fabric. However, this also presented problems. Oil paint dries by oxidation, a chemical reaction that attacks organic fibers. As a result, canvas must be sized with barrier of glue and gesso to protect it from the drying oil. It was tacked to stretchers for sizing and painting, and these sized, stretched canvases quickly replaced wood panels.

Canvas didn't warp and split like wood. It was much lighter and didn't require complex "cradling," so it could spread to cover relatively large, uninterrupted areas. Although its surface wasn't as smooth as wood, when properly prepared it received paint well and in a new way. Canvas not only supplied a woven tooth, which provided a broken texture when paint was dragged across it, but it "gave" under the brush: its spring resisted and enhanced the brush's spring. This added enormously to the possibilities of painterly touch. Oil paint, stretched canvas, and a variety of springy brushes became one of the most successful material combinations in the history of art. Today, after five centuries of use, canvas remains the primary support for painting in both oil and acrylic.

Because canvas doesn't stretch easily around complex shapes, picture shapes that derived from sculpture or architecture (for example, cruciforms or Gothic arches) declined. Large oil paintings seldom fully occupied walls: they were framed and placed upon them. Similarly, pictures no longer had to be combined in compartments or cabinets to create large-scale effects, as had been the case with earlier altarpieces.

The self-contained rectangle wasn't new to pictorial art; nevertheless, stretched canvas reinforced it powerfully. Easel paintings tended to unify within their borders rather than across the divisions of altarpieces or in relation to the shape and confines of rooms. As a result, paintings ceased to be sequences or compartments of representations (perhaps Michelangelo's Sistine ceiling was a late and supreme example of this). The unbroken surface of stretched canvas insisted on pictorial unity, a unity that took place within the confines of a harmoniously proportioned rectangle (i.e., one not too long and narrow; standardized proportions such as the Golden Section became common). In terms of representation, this unity insisted upon a coherent, illusionistic space seen at a moment of time from a singular point of view; and a unified dramatic action, or narrative.

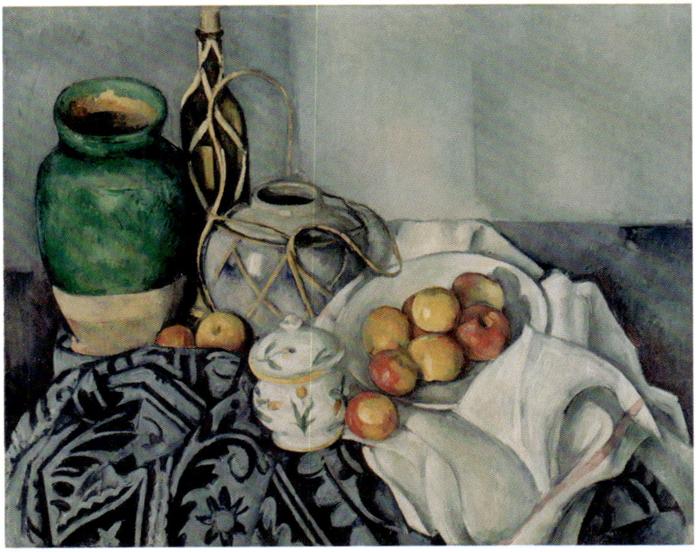

Paul Cézanne (French 1839-1906), *Still Life with Apples*, 1893-94.
Oil on canvas, 25 ¾ x 32 ⅛ in. The J. Paul Getty Museum
Photograph © 2009 The J. Paul Getty Trust

Stretched canvas brought another kind of freedom to Western painting. Because it was light and portable, relatively large paintings didn't have to be painted *in situ*. They could be painted in studios (usually on easels, hence easel painting), and the finished works could then be transported to patrons or customers with relative ease. Thus, the stretched canvas easel painting tended to replace all but the smallest panels and all but the largest frescos. This portability reinforced the reliance on standardized formats.

Paint Handling / *Facture*

Because of its thick, greasy consistency, and because it dried slowly, oil paint could be worked, corrected, and blended right on the picture surface. It could also be applied in thick, opaque layers. These heavy impastos literally raised the surface into a kind of brushed, low relief. This characteristic was enhanced in the 19th Century, when the addition of thicker oils (such as poppy seed oil) to the vehicle gave the paint a buttery consistency that held its shape as it dried. Thereafter, oil paint could be literally troweled onto the surface.

Before the development of oil paint, artistic style was defined primarily by the drawing of shapes and contours. After its introduction, and especially after the introduction of stretched canvas, expressive paint handling and brushwork were added to this. The great art historian, Heinrich Wölfflin referred to this as the "painterly" style, as opposed to the more clear-cut "linear" style. While he applied the terms to drawing, printmaking, and architecture, they clearly derived from the ascendance of oil painting. He maintained, "The Venetian school, as a whole, is the painterly school as contrasted with the Florentine."[4] To a great extent, the difference between the two schools had to do with oil paint. The Florentines in the 15th Century were slow to accept it. By the 16th Century, the Venetians had not only accepted it, but found new ways of exploiting it, laying the foundations for El Greco and Velasquez, Rubens, Rembrandt and Hals, Reynolds, Gainsborough, and Constable, Delacroix, Manet, Monet, and Cézanne.

Some years ago I suggested to the painter, Kenneth Noland, that Titian was probably the greatest oil painter. "No," he replied, "Cézanne was." His quick response struck me forcibly. In a sense we were both right: they were bookends to a library of great masters.

Watercolour

Watercolour, as we know it today, was taken up and developed in England in the late 18th Century as a means of making tinted drawings directly from nature. As Delacroix suggested, it was and remains an airy English medium: an easily portable, waterborne paint used in combination with appropriate paper. Watercolour consists of finely ground pigment applied in transparent washes. Its whites and highlights tend to be "reserved" after the practice of wash drawing, presented by the paper itself rather than by additions of opaque white paint. In the mid-18th Century, watercolours were essentially tinted drawings. When William Reeves introduced cake watercolours in the 1880s, its colour resources expanded substantially. The great age of English watercolour began. In the hands of masters like Thomas Girtin (1775-1802), J. M. W. Turner (1775-1851), John Sell Cotman (1782-1842), and Richard Parkes Bonington (1802-28) it became a medium of power and flexibility.

Drawing, usually in pencil or some similar graphic medium, has been the traditional foundation of watercolour: lightness is all, for drawing leaves traces, sometimes subtle, which can be seen through the transparent washes. The great English watercolour painters tended to be "drawing masters." One can scarcely tell where Girtin's pencil ends and his brush begins; Cotman's subtle divisions seem to detach from their subjects; Turner's drawing often floats above his washes.

In concert with contemporary poetry, watercolour explored "picturesque" and "sublime" subjects. In the late 18th Century, abbeys and gothic ruins abounded, as

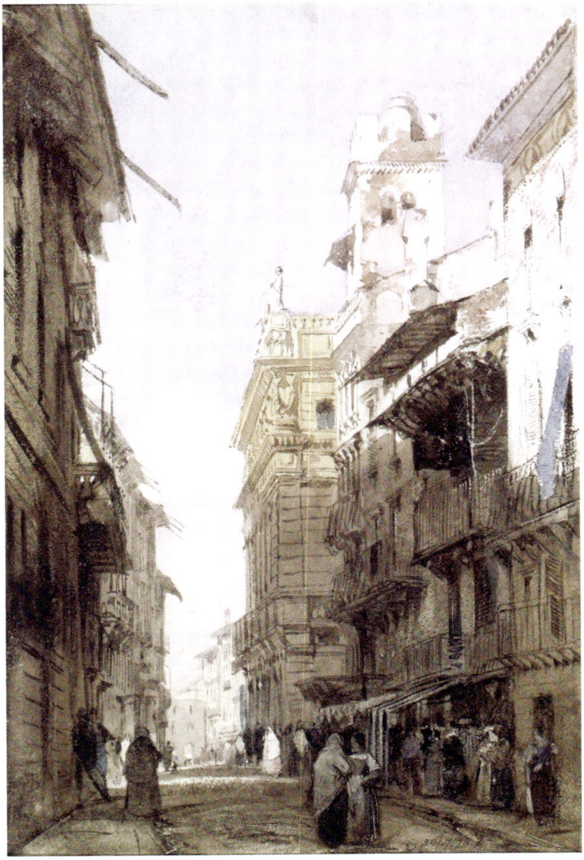

Richard Parkes Bonington (English 1802-1828), *Corso Sant'Anastasia, Verona, with the Palace of Prince Maffei*, 1826.
Watercolour, 9 ¼ x 6 ¼ in. Victoria and Albert Museum. London
Photograph © Victoria and Albert Museum, London

I saw a tall adolescent making watercolour studies after Flemish landscapes. Already in this genre, which was an English novelty at the time, he had an astonishing ability.

— Eugene Delacroix on Richard Parkes Bonington

did "shooting torrents" and "black drizzling crags," but these were tempered by more homely subjects, as in *The Task* by William Cowper:

> Here Ouse, slow winding through a level plain
> Of spacious meads with cattle sprinkled o'er,
> Conducts the eye along its sinuous course
> Delighted.

During the golden age of British landscape painting the French Revolution and Napoleonic wars shut off her artists from Europe. (Turner made a famous trip the French Alps during the brief Peace of Amiens in 1802). As a result, the British landscape school—and watercolour in particular—developed along independent lines, which explains why the "English novelty" struck Delacroix so forcefully when he encountered Bonington in the 1820s.

Despite Delacroix and even Cézanne, watercolour never took root on the continent. The great British influence on French art came, instead, from Constable's oils, which inspired the Barbizons and through them the Impressionists. Ironically, England was slow to accept Constable during his lifetime, and acceptance was impeded even after his death by John Ruskin's critical disdain.

Painting in watercolour continued to develop in England throughout the 19th Century. Unfortunately, many painters sought to demonstrate that watercolour was as "worthy" a medium as oil. They painted meticulous "exhibition watercolours" in the studio, often imitating the effects of oil paint. Technically impressive though these were, they were a symptom of decline. After about 1830 the great age of watercolour had passed. Girtin died in 1802, Bonington in 1828; Samuel Palmer's vision subsided; Turner succumbed to the vapors; and, overwhelmed by Turner's fame, Cotman took to imitating the effects of oils. The next great revival of landscape painting belonged to France.

To be sure, the British watercolour tradition didn't die out altogether. Artists as substantial as Peter deWint and David Cox soldiered on. Like a hidden stream it nourished artists throughout the English-speaking world well into the 20th Century. It came to English Canada in the 19th Century brought by successive waves of British immigrants, and in the 20th to the Canadian West by numerous artists, among them Inglis Sheldon-Williams, A. C. Leighton, and Walter J. Phillips.

Acrylic Paint

Is it any accident that the abstraction that emerged in the 1960s with the new acrylic paints, was in its infancy, a schematic "linear" style? The answer is a qualified yes, though the parallel isn't exact. Oil paint emerged against a background of tempera and fresco and at first glazed over their schematic character. On the other hand, acrylic emerged in the shadow of oil paint, but initially with few of its properties. It was schematic somewhat of necessity.

But the analogue was by no means perfect. Acrylic had advantages and disadvantages. It answered a need initiated by Jackson Pollock for a relatively liquid paint that could enable large-scale painting. Early acrylic paint was thinned with solvent and was applied in washes directly into the weave of canvas like a permanent watercolour. Because solvents posed a serious health risk, the paint was reformulated to be thinned with water. Large-scale acrylics were often painted, as Pollock had with his "drip" paintings, on unstretched canvas laid out on the floor (although Morris Louis and Larry Poons poured paint down upright surfaces.) These paintings were cropped, stretched, and framed after the paint dried. Picture shape often came last.

By the 1970s, under pressure from artists, chemistry found ways to achieve a painterly analogue of oil paint. The introduction of gels and modeling pastes enabled painting on a large scale with thickly manipulated paint.

Surface

Different kinds of pictures have different surfaces and these surfaces interact with picture-content in different ways. Paintings are the most familiar kind and in some respects the richest, because the paint surface—especially in oil or acrylic—is so variable, ranging from thin semi transparent washes to thick impastos. There's always an interaction in paintings between the support—panel, paper, canvas most frequently—and the paint application. This is part and parcel of the expressive capacities of the different media.

Photographs are something else altogether. Attempts to give a surface to photographs (apart, possibly, from some gravures) have tended to be counter-productive. A photograph lacks the material specificity of painting. It can be enlarged (within limits) and shown on screens with little loss of expression. This doesn't mean that the medium is inferior, only different.

PICTURE TYPES & THEIR SUBJECTS

Devotional Paintings and Frames

In the 14th Century, the church and aristocracy ceased to be the sole patrons of artists and illuminators. The growth of cities and a growing middle class brought a demand for religious images that could be displayed in the home along with breviaries and prayer books. This gave rise to small panel pictures. These were framed, often in semi-architectural ways derived from the borders surrounding illustrations in manuscripts as well as church mouldings. They were initially painted in egg tempera, after the fashion of illumination. In fact, many of the early panel painters were also illuminators.

The picture frame was new to European art. As it both separated the contained image from its surroundings (usually a wall) and protected it from damage, it came to have a decisive effect on the development of pictures. Frames today continue to observe both of these functions.

Perspectives

In the 14th Century, the horizon replaced the ground plane as a stabilizing and governing device in painting. Whereas the ground plane echoed and reinforced only the bottom edge of the image, the horizon—even when it was only implied—mediated between top and bottom. It echoed and reinforced the containing picture shape. Subsequently, pictures increasingly inclined to the rectangular format that we're familiar with today.

This didn't happen overnight. The rectangle was used more commonly with narratives from the Gospels, pictures depicting an event. Single figures, often images of saints, were set in panels that suggested gothic niches. They were slower to adopt the vertical rectangle that was to become the standard "portrait" format.

Two kinds of perspective were contingent upon the discovery of the horizon:

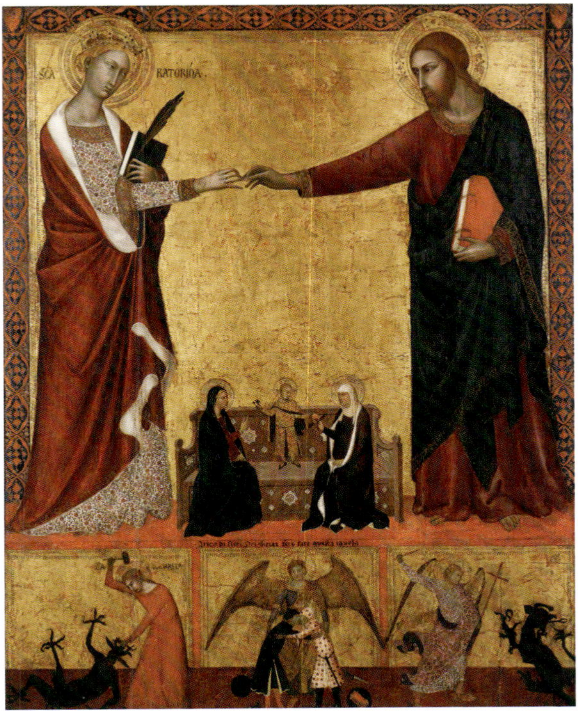

Barna da Siena (Italian, active ca. 1330-1350), *The Mystic Marriage of St. Catherine*, c. 1340. Tempera on panel 54⅝ x 43¾ in. Museum of Fine Arts, Boston, Sarah Wyman Whitman Fund. Photograph © 2009 Museum of Fine Arts, Boston

AERIAL PERSPECTIVE emerged in Flanders in the 15th Century assisted by the blending and glazing properties of oil paint. It suggested the illusion of distance through fading colour and cool tonalities as land receded towards the horizon.

LINEAR PERSPECTIVE developed in Italy around the same time. The geometry of recession in space was discovered in 1415 by the Florentine architect Filippo Brunelleschi. He found that a vanishing point converging at the horizon accounted for the illusion of diminishing size as objects receded from view. In the 15th Century Italian artists seized upon linear perspective as an aid to composition. It offered a "science" of pictorial unity, especially in compositions with rectilinear architecture or checkerboard floors. By the 16th Century perspective was adopted universally, albeit more subtly, into the methods of European artists.

This is an outstanding example of the ability of oil paint to suggest the play of light on textures as well as to suggest character. Titian was a pioneer in using the substance of thickened oil paint. The picture is all colour and brushwork, which under Titian's brush become velvet, linen, and fur. How did he do it? Pictures like these set the tone for portraiture for centuries to come and are among the glories of Western art. As a study of character given pictorial presence, the picture comes to exemplify the person.

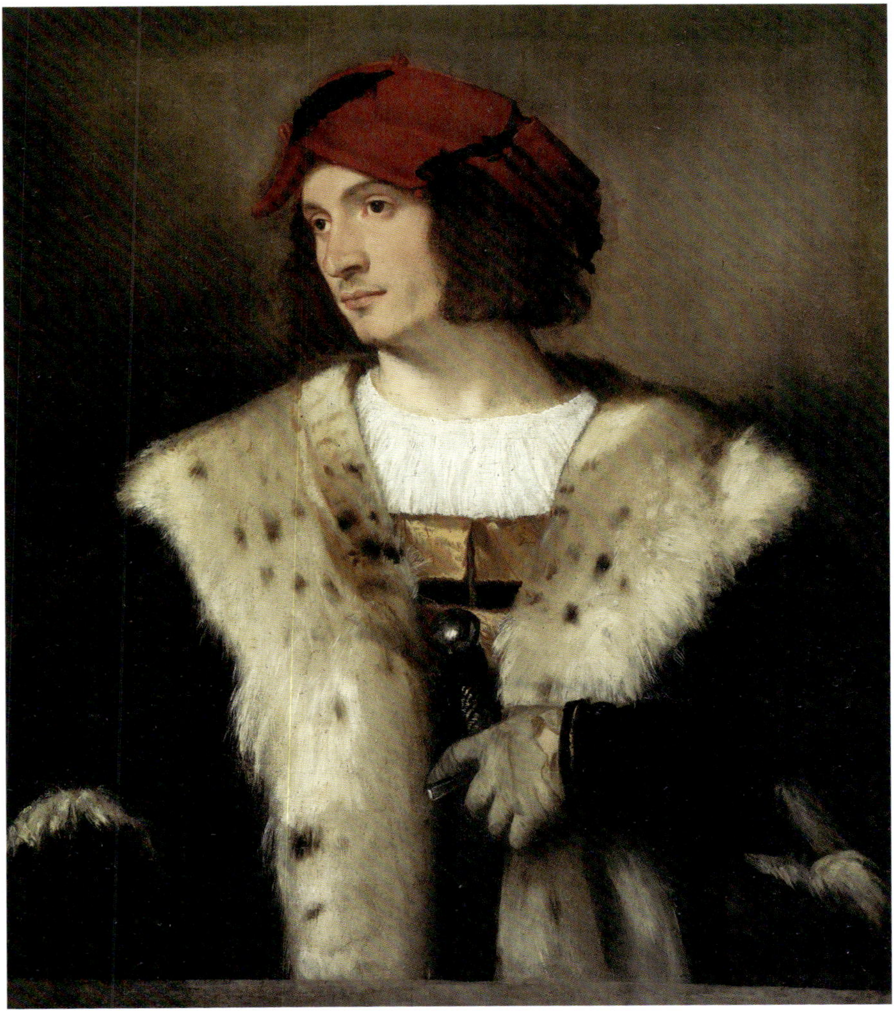

Titian (Tiziano Vecellio, Italian 1485-1576), Portrait of a Man in a Red Cap, 1516.
Oil on canvas, 32⅜ in. x 28 in. The Frick Museum, Henry Clay Frick bequest.
Photograph © The Frick Collection, New York

Easel Picture

Between 1500 and 1950 the primary vehicle of pictorial development in the West was the easel picture. It developed within the confines of an art that was boldly and fundamentally representational.

During the 15th Century, pictures became more and more self-contained. Within their borders they tended to represent figures set in a coherent space seen from a single point of view. Even when depictions multiplied in altarpieces the individual units tended to be self-contained pictures.

In the 16th Century, the unities of narrative and representation were reinforced by the material unity of oil paint and the easel picture, a material unity that began and ended inside the picture frame. These unities called for spatial coherence. Prior to 1500, painting had exploited emphatic patterns and clearly drawn shapes. But these, even when supplied by geometric perspective, tended to interrupt the picture surface and undermine its integral wholeness. Oil paint reemphasized this wholeness by blending and blurring, and by suggesting an enveloping atmosphere. Chiaroscuro, which gave strong effects of relief by modeling with darks and lights, gave way to sfumato and various other methods of surrounding figures with atmosphere by blending them into the paint surface. This unity of setting and atmosphere led, eventually, to the "pure" landscape painting of the 17th Century. In a sense, this was a precursor of art for art's sake, a kind of pictorialism for its own sake: the "picturesque." In the latter 19th Century, the Impressionists exploited the alliance between pictorial unity and landscape once again. This time it led away from representation.

Michelangelo was a curious exception to Renaissance pictorialism. In his paintings he tended to compose in terms of the single figure or figure group rather than the picture as a whole. While this resulted in some of the supreme achievements of Western art, it belonged, in that one respect, to the Medieval and Byzantine past. Even his late paintings aren't quite pictorial units, at least not in the sense of the Raphael's, and a sense of place in them is scarcely more than suggested. The spatial dislocations of Michelangelo's late Mannerism may well stem from a tendency to carry Medieval figure units into the pictorial world of Raphael and Titian.

Some Baroque painters countered this tendency towards the contained easel picture, but generally when they conceived in large, architectural units. For example some Italian ceiling painting sought to extend and unify the entire interior space. But the very fact that it tended to dissolve figures in clouds, sky, and light suggests that Venetian oil painting—and painterly unity—had intervened.

Portraits

There are many kinds of pictures, and among them many overlaps with other images and image complexes. An early and curiously illuminating example is the portrait. As a depiction of likeness and character, the portrait didn't become fully pictorialized until the 15th Century, with the emergence of the three quarter view and the ability of oil paint to capture the illusion of an external light source.

It's true that portraits were often commissioned to record and flatter society patrons. But why have so many of them turned out to be masterpieces? The influence of humanism alone doesn't answer enough for the portrait's illustrious career in Western art.

The portrait is generally a simple figure-ground composition arranging one complex shape in a shallow space related to and bounded by a vertical picture rectangle. Prior to this, portraiture had been confined in sculpture to the Roman portrait bust and in painting to the funerary images from Fayuum in Roman Egypt rendered in encaustic. But for all their startling likeness, the latter are pictures only incidentally and, as it were, after the fact, having been painted to adorn coffins. (They were painted on irregularly shaped panels, made to fit within a roughly oval aperture.) Byzantine icons also used the portrait format in a semi-pictorial way. But these tended to be enclosed images, similar to the funerary portraits from Fayuum: quasi-pictures, "almost" pictures.

Italian artists struggled with the portrait in the 15th Century, but it took them some time to find an alternative to likeness in profile. Profile portraits were closely related to the bas-relief of medallions (which survive today as the "heads" in coinage.) They provide some sense of physiognomy, but no sense of encounter or personality. The three-quarter view emerged first in Flanders with Jan van Eyck. It proved to be quintessentially pictorial, presenting the illusion of an encounter with a real person. It had much to do with the representation of eyes and flesh, often reinforced by hands, which interacted with the picture rectangle.

In the developed portrait, figure and ground participate in a new way. The figure is related integrally within an illusionistic space. The background, no matter how vague, participates in the aesthetic effect. To separate figure from ground is unthinkable. We encounter a painted portrait much as we would a person, and this sense of presence accounts for the endurance of the genre. "Character" and rectangular presence: for five centuries a fruitful aesthetic partnership.

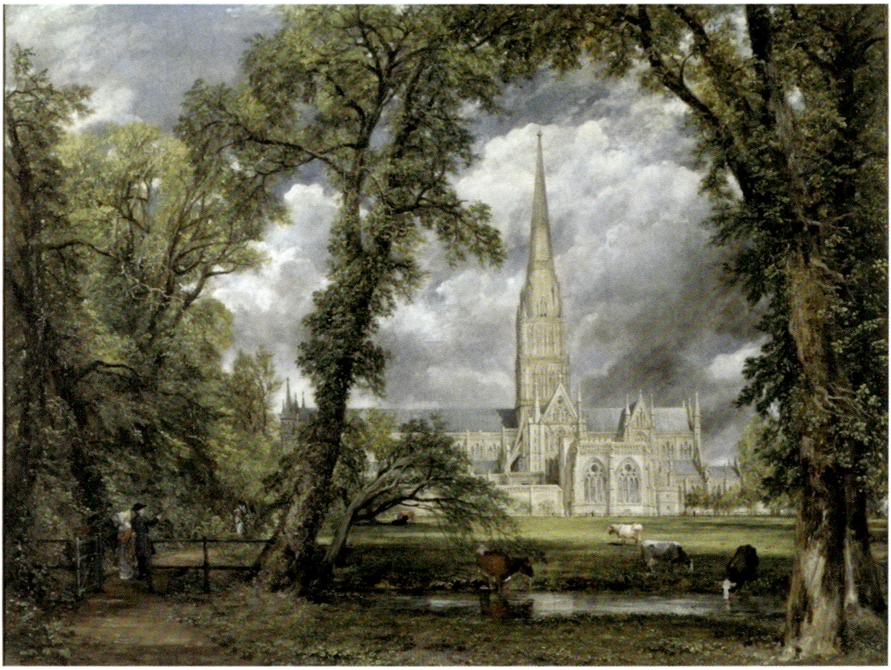

John Constable (English 1776-1837), *Salisbury Cathedral from the Bishop's Ground*, 1823.
Oil on canvas, 34½ x 44 in. The Victoria and Albert Museum
Photograph © Victoria and Albert Museum, London

Landscape

Although landscape painting emerged later than the portrait and pictorial narrative, it had a long and significant gestation. So long as discrete images were set in loose relation to one another, or attached in frieze-fashion to a ground plane, landscape was of little consequence. But when unity across a defined surface grew in importance, the depiction of an environment became one means of achieving it: landscape as a specific, coherent background eventually emerged as a subject in and of itself; in effect, the background became the picture. Eventually, landscape painting became closely identified with the picture *as* a picture.

In the 17th Century, the "classical" landscapes of Claude Lorraine and the Poussins and the more pastoral subjects of Dutch and Flemish painters—Hobbema, Ruisdale,

Cuyp—led to an English taste for "picturesque" landscape subjects in the 18th Century.

The picturesque found beauty in natural subjects with a painterly aspect. It made possible the English estate garden that remains of seminal importance to gardening on a large scale. The picturesque, wedded to the more grandiose "sublime," led to a taste for untamed scenery and eventually to the setting aside of such natural areas as protected parks. I suspect that today's national parks would be inconceivable apart from the picture as a category and landscape painting as a particular and essential manifestation of it. Constable's painting of *Salisbury Cathedral* was painted in this tradition. Unlike St. Francis in Bellini's masterpiece, the gentleman depicted—perhaps a drawing master—is pointing out a picturesque "view" to a young lady; he isn't embracing the entire visible world.

By the mid 19th Century the development of oil paint in tubes, new "industrial" pigments, and increased access to the country offered by railroads paved the way for the French Barbizon painters and the Impressionists. For the first time artists were able to paint easel pictures directly from nature. By the 1870s, landscape had become the paramount focus for ambitious artists. The great Impressionist paintings from this period were begun (and sometimes finished) out of doors. Painting *en plein air* for the Impressionists and their followers became a norm, and left masterpieces of world art. Landscape painting appeared to decline in the 20th Century, but that may be just an appearance. The Fauve-Postimpressionist tradition of landscape painting retained a kind of underground vitality throughout the century.

In 20th Century Canada, the Group of Seven took advantage of an expanding national rail system to present a complex vision of an enormous new country. After World War II, the automobile, and the roads that accommodated it, increased access to landscape subjects, both distant and near. In recent years landscape painters have been able to travel widely and work virtually from portable studios out of minivans. This portability has enabled them to work from nature on a generous scale.

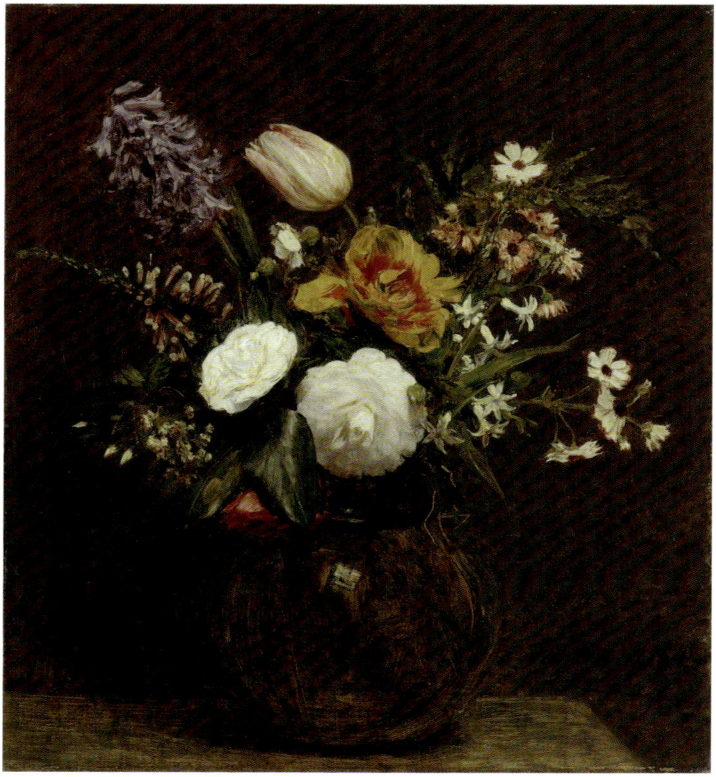

Henri Fantin-Latour (French 1836-1904), Flowers: *Tulips, Camellias, and Hyacinths*, 1864.
Oil on canvas, 19½ x 17½ in. Victoria and Albert Museum.
Photograph © Victoria and Albert Museum, London

Still Life

I suspect that still life is ancient genre, often a part of figure representations in classical art. In manuscript illumination decorative borders often contained still life elements. But the genre came into its own emphatically with the framed picture. In the hands of some painters—notably Chardin and Cézanne—it produced masterpieces.

Roger Fry remarked once that it wasn't favoured by the English because it lacked significant subject matter, was too close to "pure painting" for a literary culture. Maybe so. But the English liked Fantin-Latour, perhaps because he was so adept at suggesting flowers with paint.

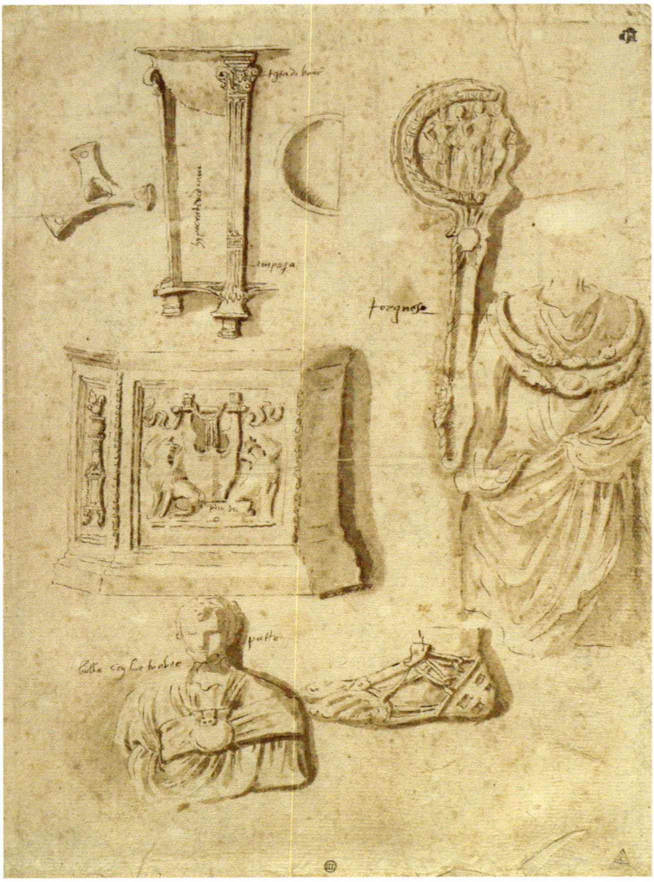

Nicolas Poussin (French 1594–1665.) French, Rome, about 1645.
Pen and brown ink and brown wash, 10⁹⁄₁₆ x 7¾ in. The J. Paul Getty Museum

Sketch

Paper made possible sketches, studies, and preliminary drawings. These weren't necessarily pictures in themselves, as they often consisted of picture fragments: faces, hands, etc. In a sense they brought the medieval pattern book closer to observed life.

The sketch also encouraged rapid, on-the-spot notation. John Constable, for example, did large preliminary studies on canvas for his more finished salon paintings. (These studies questioned the notion of "finish," which helps to explain Ruskin's aversion to them.) The Impressionists brought the seeming spontaneity of the sketch to the fore. They replaced "finish" with colour and a more immediate paint surface.

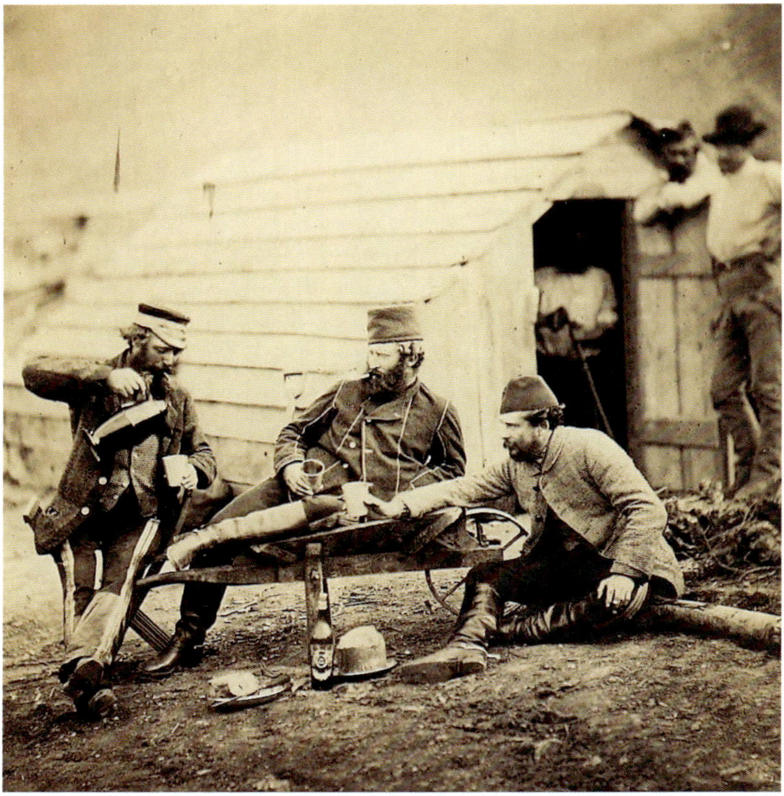

Roger Fenton, (English 1819-1861) *Hardships in the Camp (Colonel Lowe and Captains Brown and George)*, Crimea, Ukraine, 1855.
Salted paper print from glass negative, 6⅞ x 6¼ in.
Photograph © Victoria and Albert Museum, London

When photography emerged in the 19th Century it became an adjunct to the sketch from nature. By the late 20th Century, photographs had all but replaced sketches as studies for paintings. Today, many painters who work in the studio from photographs continue to draw from the motif. If nothing else, it helps keep them aware of the limitations of photography.

Photography

Photography *seems* to see what the human eye sees. It uses a "camera" with a circular lens to transfer an image onto a flat, rectangular film or sensor, in effect squaring the circle. Originally, the film image was "developed" chemically as a negative and in turn transferred as a positive to paper, though recently photographs have been captured digitally. The camera devours *subjects*. It finds them wherever one can travel. Pictures captured by the camera carry such a prosaic sting of truth, it's been suggested that photography isn't an art medium at all. It is.

But much as the camera sees *what* the eyes see, it doesn't see *as* the eyes see. Our eyes see darks and lights and colour differently from a camera; they move and focus continuously and see an unbounded continuum. Our brains, in turn, interpret and filter vision in a variety of ways. The camera doesn't do that. It stops motion and frames parts of the visual field. It takes pictures. Our eyes don't.

It can be argued that the photograph, which spawned both motion pictures and television, was often used primarily to convey utilitarian information altogether apart from aesthetic value, and that in these cases accrued aesthetic value is accidental, almost in the way of unformalized aesthetic experience. Almost, but not quite. Such a photograph retains the character of immediacy as well as a host of pictorial conventions—shape, shading, perspective, figure and ground, and the like. The "information" in many such documents is reinforced by immediacy and enhanced—often powerfully—by aesthetic appeal. It's the visual equivalent of a bugle call.

One of the ironies of photography as an art medium is the fact that it seems to prefer monochrome: black or sepia and white. Colour often detracts from its aesthetic effect. This is hardly the case with painting, where the opposite is generally the case. I suspect that there are several reasons for this. Certainly the "abstraction" provided by monochrome is a factor; colour may provide a degree of information overload. Allied to both of these is the peculiar lack of "surface" of a photograph. While it can record texture and detail with remarkable fidelity, it accomplishes this remarkable feat in the absence of a literal texture of its own, at least not one that relates to depicted texture the way colour in paint is tied directly to its literal substance.

While there's obviously a "craft" to photography, one that involves exposure, definition, & print quality, a very large part of the emotive and aesthetic effect of a photograph comes from the subject it portrays, from its depiction and its associations. These are often, and perhaps most effectively, subliminal. Somehow, colour subverts this illusion, perhaps because it wants to grab the surface as decoration.

The boundary between the mere photographic copy (like an x-ray or a photocopy) and an image experienced as a picture is by no means hard and fast. Walker Evans,

Orest Semchishen, now retired from radiology and photography, should be a Canadian national treasure. For over 30 years, in the last decades of the 20th Century, he created a vast archive of images, drawn mostly from the Canadian West. Photographs like this document a moment in time that contains a little history. It suggests a story, albeit a wordless one filled with questions and ambiguities.

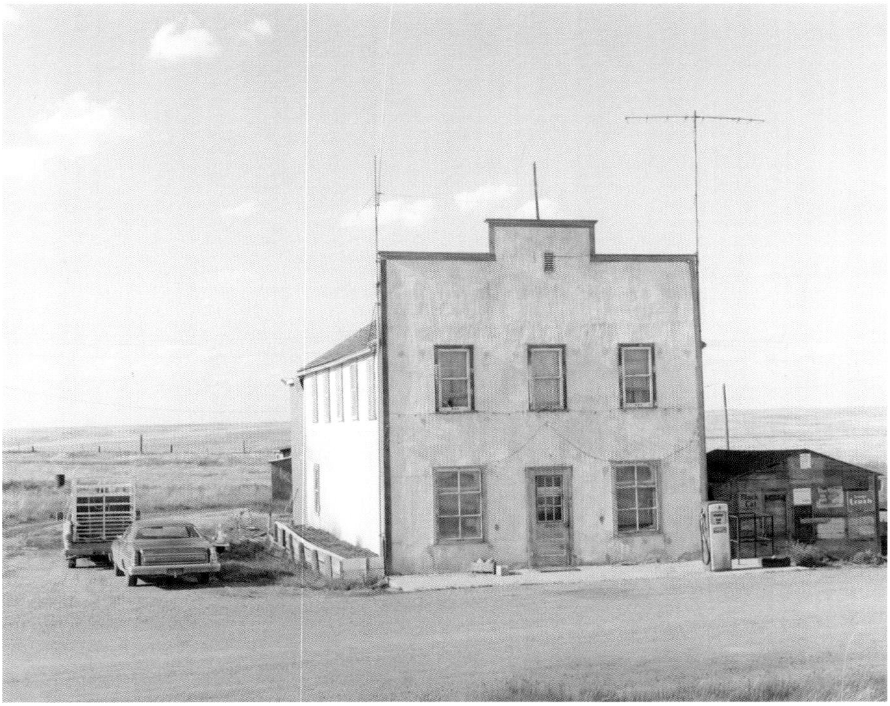

Orest Semchishen (Canadian, 1932-), *Buffalo, Alberta*, June 1979.
Courtesy of the artist.

About twenty-five years ago Wildenstein Gallery in New York mounted a benefit exhibition of the 20th Century portrait. The big names were all there: Picasso, Matisse, and a host of others. There were masterpieces. Nevertheless, I was startled, upon turning a corner into a side gallery, to encounter a photograph of the painter Otto Dix by the Surrealist, Man Ray. It offered something that the paintings hadn't, the portrayal of an individual—the traditional domain of portraiture. What had happened to the painted portrait in the 20th Century?

The exhibition seemed to demonstrate that it had changed around the turn of the century. The paintings were mostly explorations of the portrait format rather than studies of character or personality. The painting had become the thing, not the subject. Not so the photograph. Thanks to Nadar we know what Baudelaire looked like, thanks to Julia Margaret Cameron, we encounter Tennyson and Browning, sometimes as noble souls, sometimes as just people.

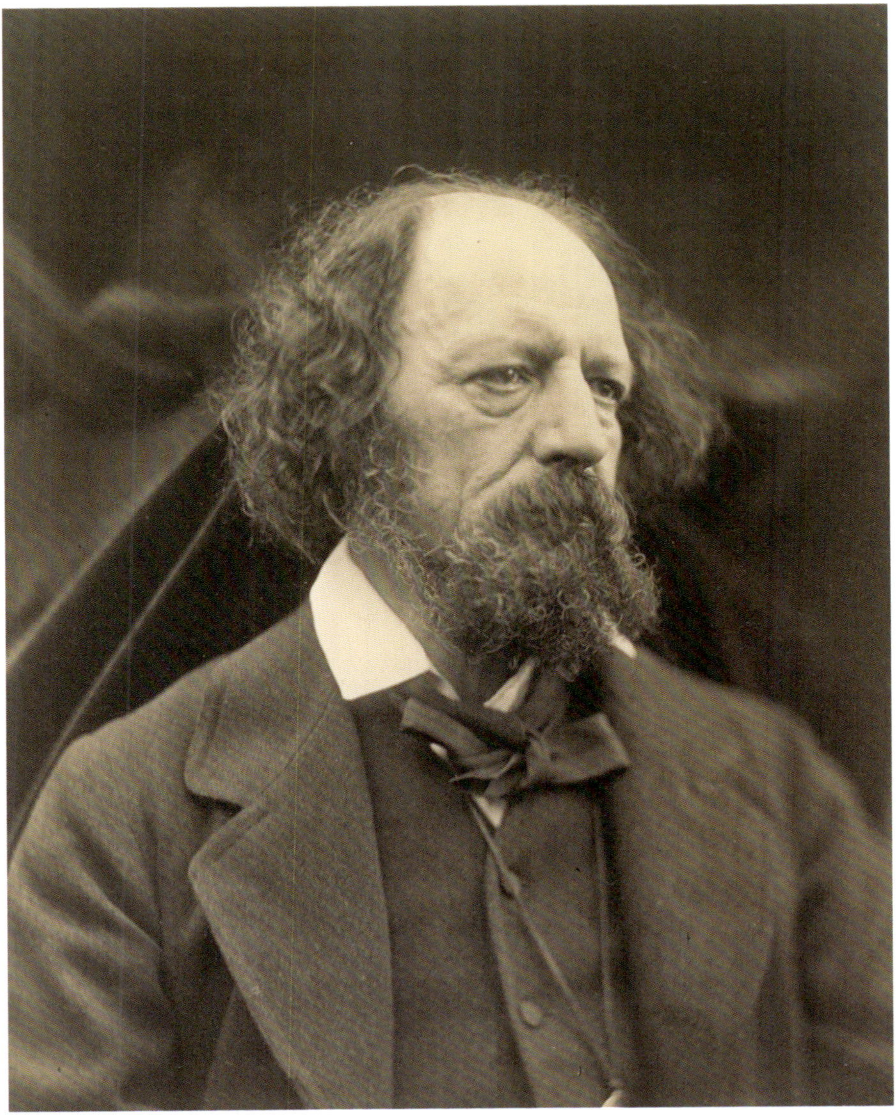

Julia Margaret Cameron (English 1815-187), *Alfred Tennyson*, 1869.
Albumen print, 12 x 9⅝ in. Victoria and Albert Museum.
Photograph © Victoria and Albert Museum, London

for example, photographed a group of images from a portrait booth. Evans and others have photographed images of signs and posters and billboards, usually with just enough context to pictorialize them. In the 1960s some of this "finding" morphed into painting and printmaking as Pop Art; Andy Warhol's famous *Campbell's Soup Tins* are a case in point. But the point was Duchampian: art by definition but aesthetically negligible; presented "ironically" as fine art; priced accordingly.

The influence of the photograph upon painting is complex and poses an unanswerable question. Did it really free artists from representation or would that have happened anyway? Whatever the case, since the mid 19th Century painting has explored its decorative "tactile" side with a vengeance. This tactile side to modern painting accomplished much. Early in the 20th Century Picasso and Matisse in their different ways made the painted picture more and more a thing in its own right: Picasso by emphasizing tactility in a literal and illusionist way; Matisse by aligning with colour and decorative pattern.

What happened to portrait painting?

Who was the last great portrait painter? Manet, Van Gogh, Cézanne, John Singer Sargent? Sargent was probably the last important artist who painted portraits on commission. The others made steps toward the portrait as pure painting. Was any of this a reaction to photography, which had become a portrait medium in the interim? Whether it was or not, by the 20th Century, photography had all but replaced painting as the primary portrait medium.

If photographs are pictures, what are motion pictures?

They're a different medium altogether; not lesser, just different. A rapid succession of "stills" creates a sensation of movement that somehow undermines the effect of a still picture. Even when the movement is glacial, as it is in many artists' videos, there's an implication that the work should be endured to the bitter end, as if "fine art" were a residual thing that remained after everything of interest or entertainment had been stripped away.

Because motion pictures take place in time, they're a kind of performance art, combining theatre and music as well as rectangular visual sequences. In a sense, they solve the problem of narrative that has frustrated visual artists for centuries.

In the past, visual artists handled narrative in a couple of ways. One, by selecting a defining moment in a narrative: an annunciation, crucifixion, or pieta, for example. Secondly, by establishing a series of events within a single frame or in adjacent frames (like contemporary comic strips.) In some cases, these were enriched with incorporated texts. But texts in pictures tend to interrupt visual coherence. For some reason (possibly neurological and psychological) still pictures reward our attention in ways that moving pictures can't.

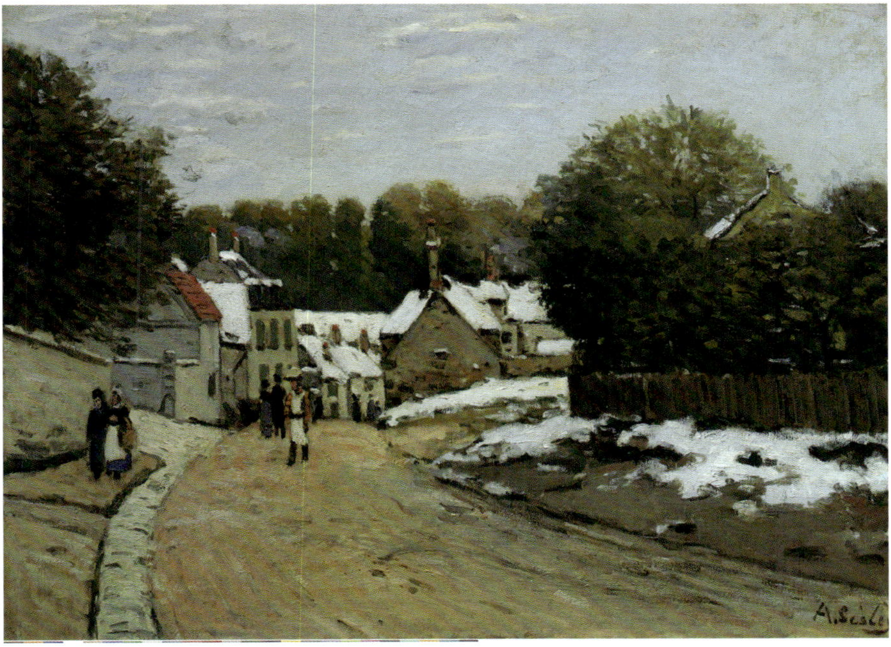

Alfred Sisley (French, born England 1839-1899), *Early Snow at Louveciennes*, c. 1870–71.
Oil on canvas, 21⅝ x 29 in. Museum of Fine Arts, Boston, Bequest of John T. Spaulding
Photograph © 2009 Museum of Fine Arts, Boston

Impressionism

The French Impressionists let in the light of day; they lifted colour out of the murk to make pictures that were fresh and airy, where colour created the illusion of light. In a sense, they brought something of the light palette of watercolour into thick-textured oil painting. The subjects that were most central to their method tended to be landscapes, though some of the artists—Manet (the great predecessor), Degas, and Renoir—painted figures. But even there the figures were rather candid, not as homely as genre painting, but avoiding grand narratives at a time when the French salons were replete with "themes" and the very big names in England were paid huge sums for large biblical and classical masterworks.

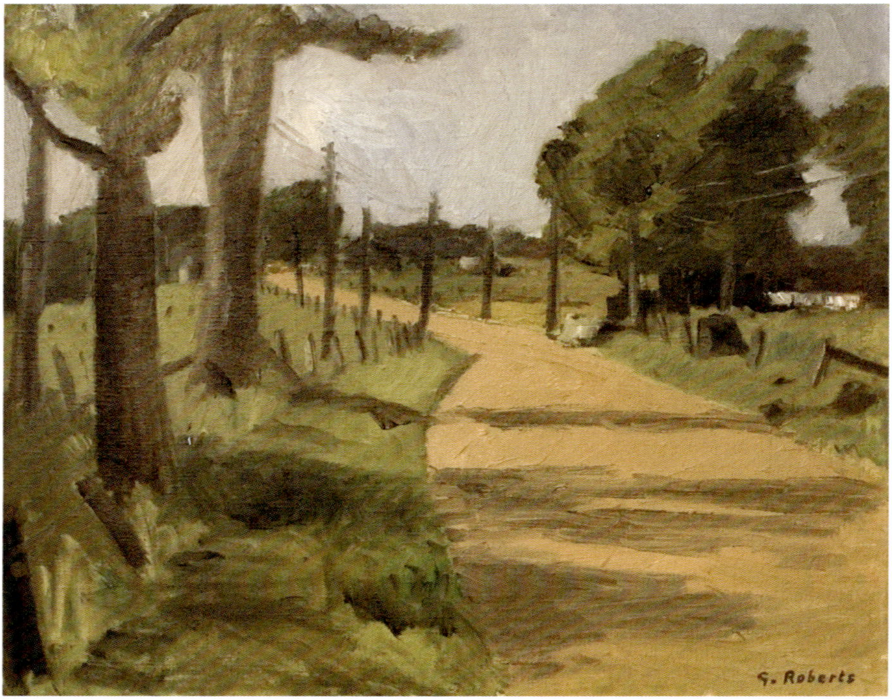

Goodridge Roberts (1904-1974), *Road in the Eastern Townships*, 1950.
Oil on canvas, 20⅞ x 26¼ in. Mendel Art Gallery, purchased with funds from the bequest of Noreen Olga Miller.
Photograph © Mendel Art Gallery, Licensed by the Goodridge Roberts Estate

Post-Impressionism / Fauvism

In the 1890s and early 20th Century, some painters began to handle Impressionist type subjects in a more blunt and forceful manner. Van Gogh and Gauguin in the 1880s, Bonnard and Vuillard in the 1890s, and the Fauves (Matisse & others) in the early 20th Century began to paint with exaggerated colours. Fauvism itself was short-lived, but the tendency to paint from nature in that straightforward manner proved to be extremely persistent. The great critic, Roger Fry, who coined the term "Post Impressionism," introduced it to England in 1910, and became its greatest apologist in the English-speaking world. In Canada, even disparate groups like the Group of Seven and the Contemporary Arts Society might fairly be called Post Impressionist. Matthew Smith, in England, Albert Marquet in France, Goodridge Roberts in Canada, and Fairfield Porter in the United States are Postimpressionists in this sense. It accounts for a broad undercurrent of ambitious representational art in the 20th Century that was to some extent overshadowed by Cubism, Surrealism, and abstraction.

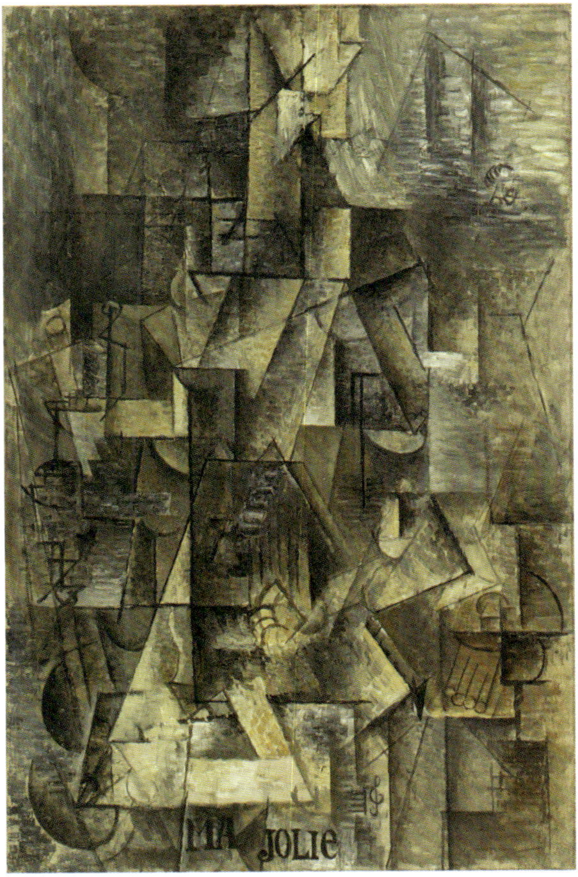

Pablo Picasso. (Spanish, 1881-1973). *Ma Jolie*. 1911-12.
Oil on canvas, 39⅜ x 25¾". Museum of Modern Art, New York.
Acquired through the Lillie P. Bliss Bequest.
Digital image © The Museum of Modern Art, Licensed by SCALA / Art Resource, NY

Like many of the masterpieces of Analytical Cubism, *Ma Jolie* adopts the format of the traditional portrait, but instead of a representational figure we're given an arrangement of interlocking facets and planes in browns and greys. The figure, a woman with guitar must be taken on trust. In fact many Cubist portraits and still lifes—drawn, I suspect, from Parisian café life—must be taken on trust. It's a pretext for a picture. Like most of the masterpieces of Analytical Cubism, *Ma Jolie* must be seen to be experienced: photographs can't do them justice.

Cubism

Cubism is one of the seminal movements of 20th Century art. Among other things it invented collage, led to constructive sculpture, and paved the way for abstraction. It began in 1907 after Pablo Picasso and Georges Braque were bowled over by the achievement of Cézanne in a posthumous retrospective exhibition at the *Salon d'Autumn* in Paris.

There have been many interpretations of what the early Cubists attempted, some of them silly, but the general style swept the world by 1914.

Basically, Cubism replaced the traditional conception of the picture as a window onto reality with one of the picture as a thing in itself, a flat surface organized into visual coherence. Instead of traditional perspective that opens up deep space, the Cubists organized the picture surface into a kind of implied all-over grid. Deep space was replaced by the illusion of a shallow space within the picture surface.

Picasso and Braque's "Analytical Cubism" of 1912-13 took a bold step in the direction of abstraction and the all-over picture. Both artists drew back from overt abstraction after about 1920, but the seed they planted grew to dominate ambitious painting for decades thereafter.

Abstraction and the all-over picture

In the 1950s and '60s abstract painting came to the fore. It didn't stand by itself in the limelight—that it shared with Pop Art—but it was front and centre in the museums, to be seen and perchance to be admired. (Now much of it is hidden away.) Sharing limelight with Pop Art was an aesthetic misalliance. That was rectified in the late '60s with the emergence of Minimal Art. There at last was a form of abstraction that held hands unaffectedly with Pop Art. By the late '60s minimalism and conceptualism had begun to upstage earlier varieties of abstraction. Gresham's law seems to apply in the contemporary art world.

At that time the "formal" side of modernism was in the ascendant and the "surreal" very much in the background. The evidence of this was the relatively minor position afforded Pop artists in the massive *Three Decades of American Painting* mounted by the Metropolitan Museum in New York in 1969. Perhaps that exhibition rang the death knell for abstraction. It's high profile declined in the 1970s, although artists who had emerged in the '50s and '60s continued to mount major exhibitions. By the 1980s the surrealist/post-modernist tradition occupied centre stage in the museums and magazines.

What's missed is the high aesthetic achievement of many, a list that includes Helen Frankenthaler, Adolph Gottlieb, Robert Motherwell, Morris Louis, Kenneth Noland, Jules Olitski, Larry Poons, Darby Bannard, Stanley Boxer, Dan Christensen, John Griefen, Larry Zox, Darryl Hughto, Susan Roth, and the Canadians Jack Bush, Bill Perehudoff, Douglas Haynes, Terrence Keller, and Robert Christie. I've overlooked several. Some had short careers, others long. Unfortunately their work is hard to see in museums these days, and emerging abstract painters suffer as a result.

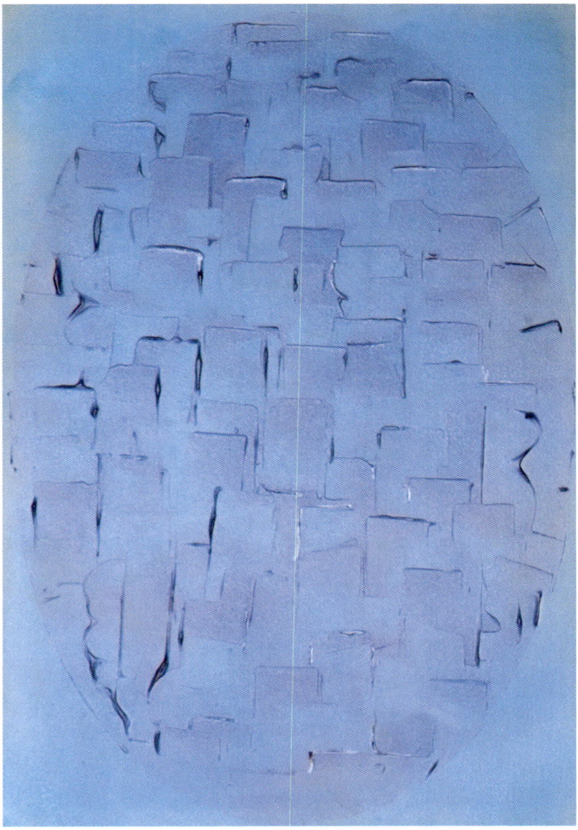

Douglas Haynes (Canadian 1936-), *Nirvana*, 1983.
Acrylic on Canvas, 54 x 37 in. The Mendel Art Gallery, Saskatoon, Canada
Photograph © The Mendel Art Gallery

Piet Mondrian came to Paris from the Netherlands in 1912 and stayed until 1914. While there he discovered Analytical Cubism. By 1913 he was painting outstanding paintings of his own based upon the work of Picasso and Braque, though more fully abstract. Several of his pictures from this period made use of an oval motif within the picture rectangle. The oval not only "contained" a grid-like cubist arrangement of lines and cells; it also emphasized its frontality and shallow space.

The Canadian, Douglas Haynes, revisited these Mondrians in 1983, but employed troweled acrylic instead brushed oil paint, using the motifs much as Picasso and Braque had used the conventions of still life and portrait. (Haynes later went on to paint Analytical Cubist motifs using the same technique.) The results were more than mere pastiches. In revisiting the format he made it new.

Uprightness

Because easel pictures were painted with thick textured oil paint that adhered to an upright surface their orientation was predetermined: top was up, bottom down.

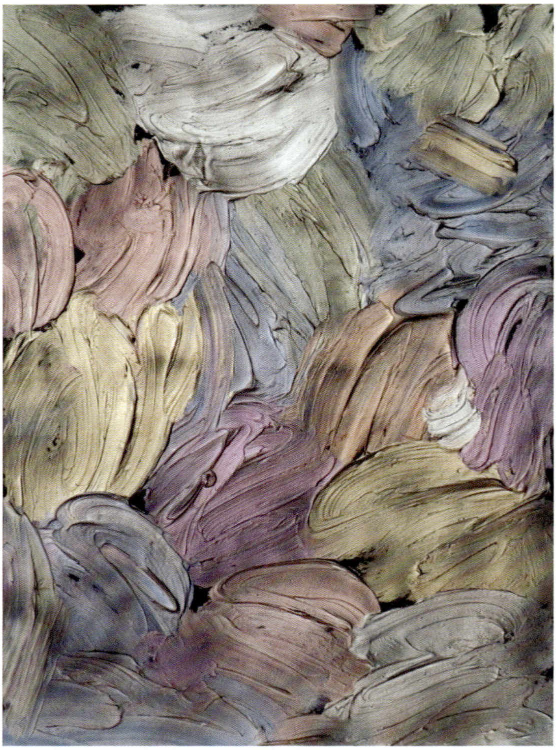

Jules Olitski (American 1922-2007), *Halcyon*, 1988.
Acrylic on canvas, 67 x 49 in. Mendel Art Gallery, gift of artist.

Jackson Pollock changed this sense of orientation by painting with liquid industrial paints on unsized canvas stapled out on the floor. Because he worked around the canvas, orientation became provisional. This isn't to say his pictures lack a top and bottom, but that their orientation was determined later, sometimes after the paintings were cropped and stretched.

After the introduction of liquid acrylics many painters continued to work like Pollock on unstretched canvas on the floor. But some took advantage of the liquidity of the paint to allow to drip and spread down sheets of upright canvas. Morris Louis used this to great effect in his "veils" and "unfurleds" from the late 1950s. Larry Poons found a new way to exploit gravity in a series of remarkable paintings from the 1970s that used the vertical striations of downward dripping acrylic to interact with the sides of his pictures.

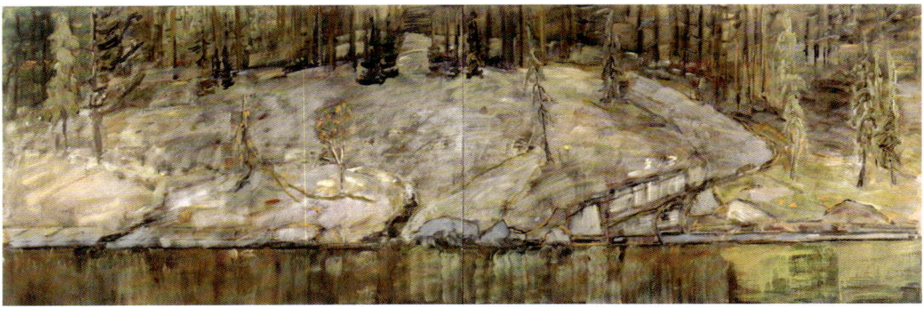

Greg Hardy (Canadian 1950-), *Quiet Bay, Rockface Diptych*, 2008.
Acrylic on Canvas, 64 x 192 in.
Photograph © Eve Kotyk
Hardy paints landscapes in the Fauve-Postimpressionist tradition, but frequently on a much-expanded scale.

The Big Picture

After World War II, artists searched for ways to get beyond the confines of the easel picture. Paintings began to increase in size. Jackson Pollock, set a new standard when he painted very large "drip" paintings in the late 1940s and early 1950s. They were painted on unstretched canvas laid out on the floor using commercial enamels and house paint. Although they had the scale of traditional murals, they were stretched and framed like traditional easel pictures. By the mid 1950s, artists like Helen Frankenthaler and Morris Louis followed Pollock's method of painting with diluted paint on a large scale. Many artists continued this practice in the 1960s, taking advantage of the new acrylic paints. Not all of their paintings were the size of portable murals, nor were all painted on unstretched canvas, but by the 1960s the general size of even easel paintings had increased. Whereas traditional easel paintings had seldom been more that four feet in their largest dimension, post war pictures were commonly six and eight feet and often much larger.

By the 1970s many abstract paintings were large in one dimension and easel picture size in their smaller one: tall verticals or long horizontals. In pictorial terms, the narrow formats tended to tie the picture illusion into the paint surface.

James Walsh's paintings aren't large; they're painted on the scale of traditional easel paintings; but they tend to use very very thick figures against thinly painted grounds. Thick paint is by no means new in recent art, but in Walsh's hands extreme relief doesn't result in semi-sculptural objects. His paintings remain eloquently pictorial.

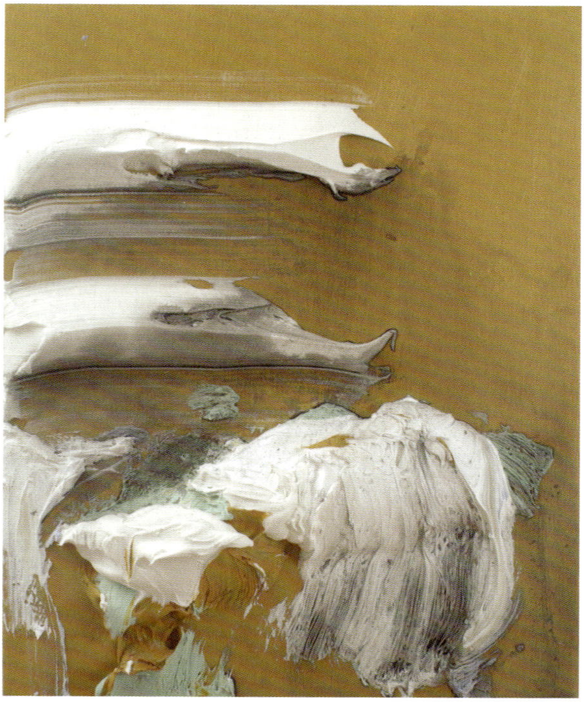

James Walsh (American 1954-), *Field Test*, 2004.
Acrylic on canvas, 27 x 22 in.
Photograph © the artist

Figure and Ground

In it's simplest sense figure and ground refers to figures in a setting, against a background. As painting became more abstract, foreground "figures" often threatened to detach from the ground, making pictures that looked thin and incomplete. There were as many solutions to the problem as there were successful painters, but three basic tendencies stood out. One was to make the "figure" occupy most of the picture surface, hence the allover painting of Jackson Pollock, Jules Olitski, Larry Poons, and more recently John Griefen. A second was to make figure and ground appear to sit side-by-side in a kind of optical space as with Adolph Gottlieb, Kenneth Noland, Jack Bush, William Perehudoff and several others. A possible third was to make the ground, itself, take over much of the picture surface with various small accents added, for example Barnet Newman and Helen Frankenthaler. Needless to say, these aren't hard and fast categories. Some painters, among them the vastly underrated Darryl Hughto, used them all.

Kenneth Noland (American 1924-), *Doors: Great Skies*, 1988. Acrylic on canvas mounted on wood with plexiglass, 81 x 46 in.
Photograph © Kenneth Noland/Licensed by VAGA, New York, NY

Shaped pictures

Before 1400, panel pictures were often shaped at the top like niches. Thereafter the rectangle dominated as it still does. From time to time some artists painted circular paintings (tondos) or ovals, but these weren't common; the shapes were inherently amorphous and unstable; the implied horizon of the post-medieval easel picture didn't suit enclosures that departed too much from the rectangle. In the early years of Cubism, Picasso, Braque, and Mondrian set ovals within some pictures, but these were generally fitted within the traditional canvas rectangle. The oval within a rectangle seemed a means to insist upon flatness and frontality.

In the 1960s, some abstract painters—notably Kenneth Noland, Frank, Stella, and Ellsworth Kelly—worked with eccentric, non-rectangular shapes. Noland, in particular, used geometry and a new kind of structural colour to generate unusual picture shapes in which the relation of external shape to internal configuration created pictorial tension.

NARRATIVE / STORYTELLING / DEMONSTRATION

Storytelling in visual art can be found on the walls of caves and in friezes and frescos dating back thousands of years. The notion that a picture is worth a thousand words confirms to my mind that visual images not only preceded writing, but also presented and preserved information in its absence. In some part, writing developed because images were inadequate for many kinds of presentation.

The building blocks of narrative art were figures and figure groups. The frieze could suggest a sequence of events (though often it didn't) or a procession. Figures and figure groups played an important role in medieval manuscript illumination, where they were often closely related to an inscribed text.

By the 14th Century, narratives had come into their own within pictures and through sequences of pictures like today's comic books. They were drawn at first from biblical events and, after the emergence of humanism, from classical and contemporary ones.

The strict confines of the framed picture both encouraged and restricted narrative. Figures and figure groups could fill pictures with action (Rubens and Delacroix specialized in this) but their sheer narrative ability was compromised by the focus on a single event. Action often called for an explanation and some kinds of action were more easily pictorialized than others.

Yet the high status of narrative persisted. In the 18th Century, Sir Joshua Reynolds maintained that "History Painting" was the highest kind of painting, although he himself excelled at portraiture. There were great examples from the Renaissance and Baroque, but when looked at closely, many didn't narrate very much. Certainly annunciations, crucifixions, and pietas abounded, but they were set pieces. Giorgione's *Tempesta*, from 1508, offered poetic enigma in place of a specific subject. In so doing he set a new standard for pictorial meaning, one that aspired, as Walter Pater put it, to "the condition of music."[5]

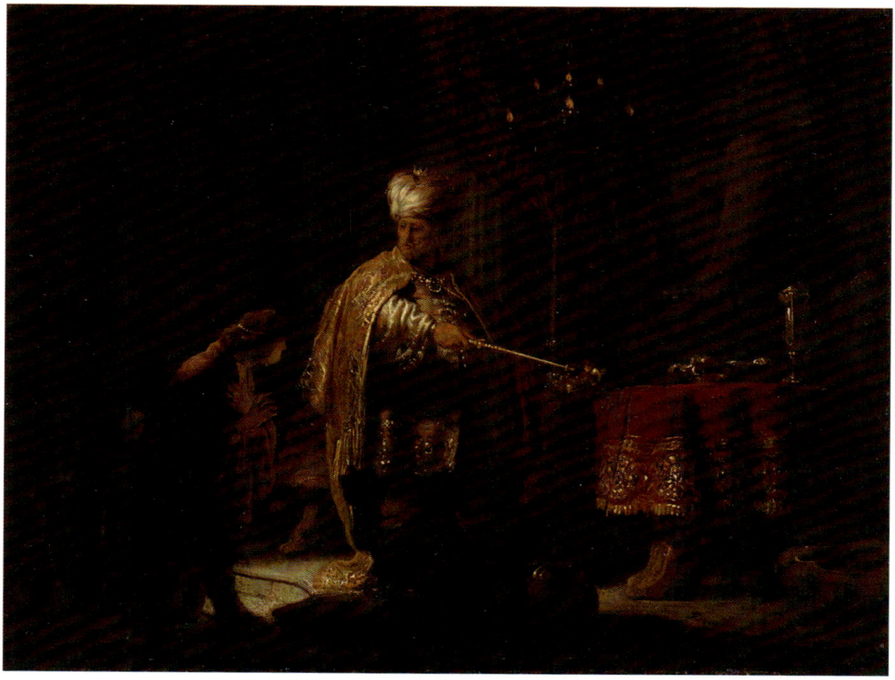

Rembrandt Harmensz van Rijn (Dutch 1606-1669), *Daniel and Cyrus before the Idol Bel,* 1633.
Oil on panel 9¼ x 11⅞ in. The J. Paul Getty Museum.
Photograph © the J. Paul Getty Trust

In the 19th Century, the conflict between narrative and pictorial completeness reached a crisis in the art of Eugene Delacroix. Delacroix painted narratives in a flamboyantly painterly manner: colour and bravura paint handling attempted to match the dramatic intensity of his exotic subjects, drawn from literature, medieval history, and, especially, North Africa. In his hands narrative inclined to violent activity: battles, lion hunts, *The Fanatics of Tangier.* As Walter Friedländer observed, he proved to be the last great narrative painter—or the last great painter obsessed with narrative. Although his rival, Jean Auguste Dominique Ingres, preached the classical style, under his brush the style had become immobile, incapable of narrating. All that remained was the statuesque pose, the statuesque portrait, and congregations of figures frozen into designs.

By the mid 19th Century, narrative had been largely relegated to the academies, the French Salons, and Victorian England. The best painters seldom took it up (I realize that van Gogh was an exception, but one that proved the rule). Eventually, even generalized human nature ceased to matter as a subject for representation. Painting inclined to

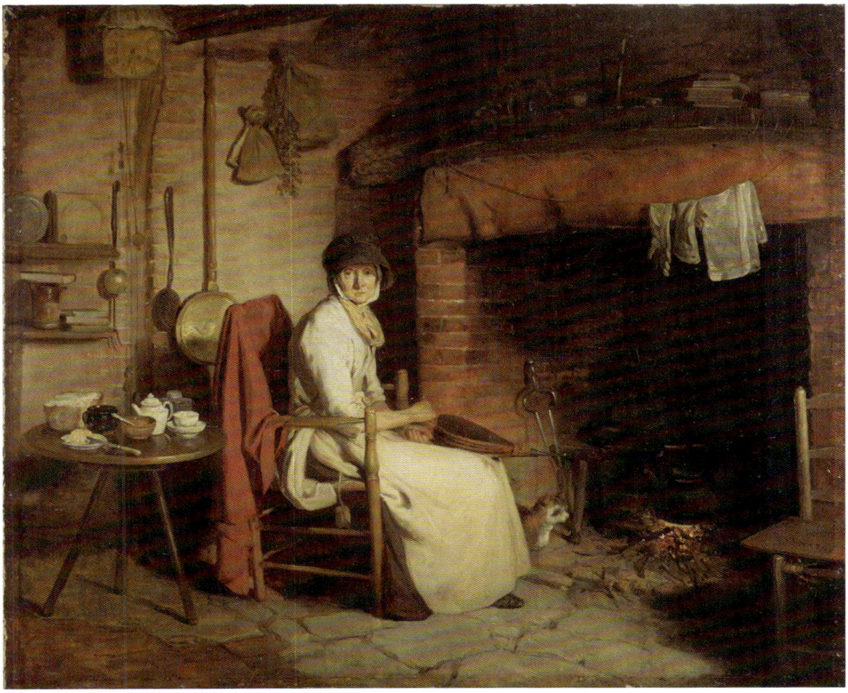

William Redmore Bigg (English 1755-1828), *Tea*, 1793.
Oil on canvas, 24 x 29 in. Victoria and Albert Museum

the exploration of its medium, to oil paint and sized, stretched canvas: to the material easel picture. In the process, it became more purely painting. Artists sacrificed unity of action, unity of time, and even unity of place to what Joshua Reynolds had called "fullness of effect." At first they abandoned coherent, unified narrative; eventually they abandoned representation itself.

Genre painting

Genre painting emerged in the Netherlands in the 17th Century and quickly spread throughout Europe. It's the obverse of history painting. Whereas history painting is often large and deals with significant events by historical personalities, genre painting tends to be small in scale and draws its subjects from everyday life. It tells homely stories. It doesn't idealize, but it does generalize and sometimes sentimentalizes. The people it depicts tend to be types rather than individuals, often the "deserving poor."

Genre of a sort flourishes in photography, but the camera, by its nature particularizes more than painting can; when it's close to the typical it still records a specific event, as such the medium carries a sting of truth that eludes painting.

Reproduction

Illustrated art books are by no means new. In the 18th and 19th Centuries they usually included mezzotints copied from original works of art. In the 20th Century the mezzotints gave way to photographic reproductions, at first in monochrome, but gradually in colour. By the 1960s, colour printing had become increasingly accurate and prevalent in magazines as well as books. These printed reproductions were augmented by colour slides (used for teaching and grant applications) and more recently by digitized images on computer screens. Today most people encounter art for the first time in reproduction. As a result, they learn about paintings from the shadow before the reality. Many who profess to know much have seen little.

The problem is complicated by the medium of photography, which translates so disarmingly well into books and onto screens.

To reproduce a painting, the reality of its paint surface must be translated into a photographic illusion. That illusion can't capture its scale and can only hint at the relation between its physical surface and its colour. Works on paper like watercolours and drawings tend to reproduce better than paintings. Illustration and Pop Art with their recognizable images and anonymous surfaces reproduce much better than colour abstraction, which in reproduction just doesn't seem *serious*. Put simply, reproduction favours pictures that reproduce well. Ones that don't, suffer.

With photography the problem of reproduction is bypassed. The reproduction of a photograph is essentially a technical problem, akin to printing in a darkroom. In a sense photography is a book or portfolio art. Photographs don't fare so well on the wall as they do in the hand or on the page.

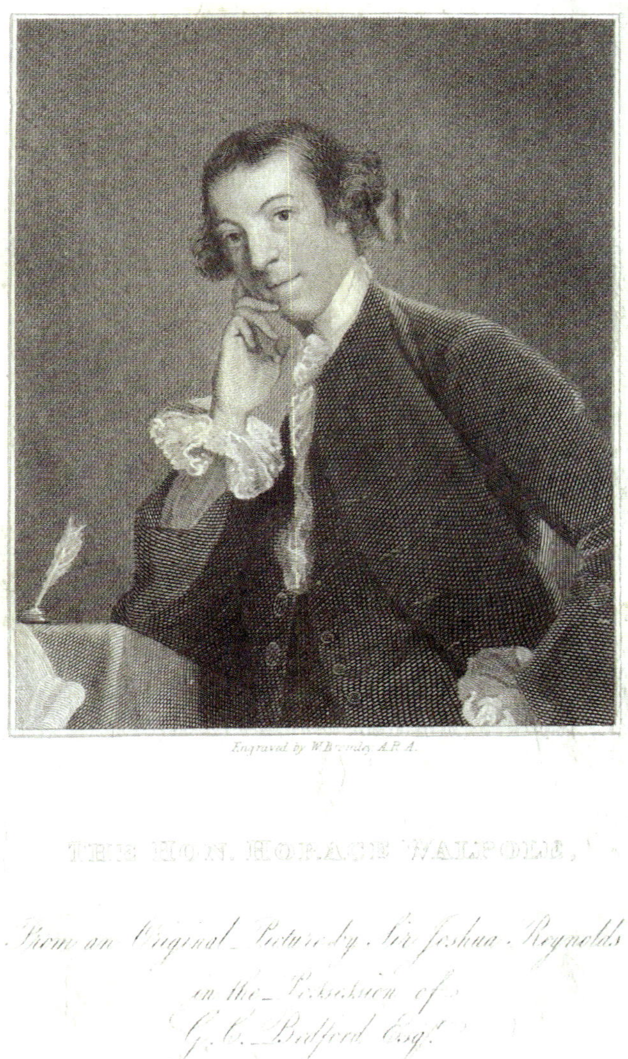

Mezzotint from Anecdotes of Painting in England by Horace Walpole from the original Mss. Of Mr. George Vertue with additions by the Rev. James Dalloway, 1828 Edition.

ART

What I dream of is an art of balance, of purity and serenity, devoid of troubling or depressing subject matter, an art which could be for every mental worker, for the businessman as well as the man of letters... a soothing, calming influence on the mind, something like a good armchair which provides relaxation from physical fatigue.[6]

—Henri Matisse

What is it?

"Art" is a category word. It refers to man made things that are intended to elicit an aesthetic response in other human beings. These are things to be *appreciated*, things that reward our attention; as Bernard Berenson put it, things that "enhance life": music and dance; stories, poems, and theatre; sculpture and pictures. We call those kinds of things "works of art."

Art appeals to a unique area of human consciousness, what might be called the aesthetic realm. It's a realm apart from, *but by no means above*, the moral and physical strictures of life, a realm of refuge where ends justify means. Its values are unique and valuable, but to maintain that they're superior to moral values is a form of barbarism. (For some, that's a hard pill to swallow.)

"Art" is a word that doesn't exist in some cultures, but that doesn't mean that aesthetic experience is absent. Most art, after all, is in some sense art for use. But the best art-for-use tends to be experienced as just-art after the use has worn off.

Unfortunately, many works of art just exemplify the category; apart from that, they don't elicit much of anything in the aesthetic realm. The reason for the category probably stems from the fact that good art exists and that lesser art is seldom bad absolutely but is less successful by shades and degrees. Much of it withers on the vine.

In the 20th Century some artists professed interest in things apart from and "above" the aesthetic realm. As a result the category expanded to include anything made by anyone who was agreed to be an artist. The question of who did the agreeing was often begged. Nowadays, art is "anything displayed in an art gallery, Q.E.D." (Check out a Whitney Biennial some time if you're in doubt.)

These days the question "what is art?" often gets invoked in arguments about freedom of expression and government funding.

That complaint aired, most artists don't try to make art by category; they try to make the best art they can—whether they're making "art for use" or what we call "fine art." Although they sometimes fail, it seems foolish to claim that their relative failures aren't art.

Anything that anyone (whether he's an artist or viewer is beside the point) wants to claim is art, is art for that person. The work might be pretentious and vapid, but that doesn't alter the fact that it's art. The important thing about art as a category is that the best of it elicits aesthetic responses in human beings. When that happens, we say things like "what a beautiful thing," sometimes to others, often just to ourselves.

Are some works of art really better than others, or is quality just a matter of personal taste?

Believe it or not some works *are* better than others within that aesthetic realm; common sense and the experience of centuries suggest that. But, because the experience of art is subjective, it can't be proved other than by pointing to a consensus over time. The fact that paintings by Leonardo and Rembrandt and Cézanne are still admired today suggests that many of their pictures *are* superior. The fact that museums and art galleries were created to care for and display pictures (and sculptures) suggests that, too. But the proof, as always, lies with your personal experience. When all is said and done only that can tell *you* what's best.

If quality were simply a matter of personal whim (not taste), everything would be equally good or bad. A painting on velvet, even a blank canvas would be as good as Bellini's *St. Francis*.

How can you tell the best works of art from lesser ones?

By looking. By comparing. By letting your own taste decide.

Remember, the good ones are seldom perfectly good, nor the bad ones utterly bad. But the better ones are more sustaining than the lesser ones.

Good art stays looking good. Mediocre art becomes something like wallpaper. Sooner or later it stops rewarding your attention. It gets taken for granted.

Good art nourishes your attention. It calls you back. It refreshes your eyes. It just looks good. All of its aesthetic "meaning" is contained in that. The real enjoyment of art comes from savoring the experience of it. Each work of art presents a different experience.

Why do we distrust art?

I'm speaking here of the English-speaking Protestant world, especially in North America, but by no means confined to that. And by Protestant, I mean by heritage and culture, not by religion. I'll begin with a quote from Henry James:

> 'Art' in our Protestant communities, where so many things have got so strangely twisted about, is supposed to be opposed in some mysterious manner to morality, to amusement, to instruction.

James wrote that in 1884. He went on to lament this mistrust of art as it applied to literature, but his initial comment stands for all the arts and the blight that Protestantism has created in the English-speaking world. As a friend once put it, "the Puritans came to the New World to escape from art and they're still running." Put more bluntly, North Americans tend to identify the arts with either sin or frivolity. Some artists rise to the bait and make art simply to provoke the Puritans.

The impact of art

A painting or sculpture communicates wherever and whenever it moves a viewer: in that alone is its impact. Of course I use the verb "move" in a special sense, as something like "the arousal of feeling," but an arousal of a specific kind, one that doesn't have to stimulate action or decision apart from the decision to report or bear witness to the stimulation itself. (I believe Kant said that.) The impact of art must be a euphemism for aesthetic communication. If it isn't, how does one account for other kinds of impact: the impact of lesser art, for example, or the impact of sensational journalism? It seems to me that impact apart from the aesthetic is impact of an altogether different kind. The impact of great art is subsumed into the aesthetic. When a different kind of impact enters art, lets say a kind of journalistic sensationalism or emotive hysteria, it often masks an aesthetic weakness.

Unfortunately, the impact of art can only be attested to. It can't adequately be described, just as the content of art can't be paraphrased. In that respect aesthetic experience is similar to religious experience. How can you describe its specific content? This is especially true of the visual arts and music, the so-called abstract arts, but at bottom it's no less true of literature. What is *Macbeth* really about; why does it move us so? Its impact on life is undeniable, but its specific character dissolves into a mystery.

Really good pictures come across as presentations, as gifts. Lesser ones are more like demonstrations.

Seeing pictures

What's the difference between experiencing a picture as a picture and perceiving other visual phenomena? Do some people just see the subject matter without experiencing the picture aesthetically? Conversely, do some people recognize a thing as a picture without experiencing it aesthetically? Could there be a neurological answer to these questions?

In a sense, the difference between a collection of images and a picture is analogous to the difference between poetry and prose. The boundary isn't hard and fast, but despite the overlap, there's a general distinction.

Speaking for myself, when I see a picture as a picture, it comes together in my mind with a kind of click—a metaphorical click. Some good pictures look like painted objects at first; the click doesn't happen right away. Some pictures are irritating at first; history seems to suggest that. It's as if they're written in a foreign language but contain within themselves the keys to its translation.

The Emperor's New Clothes

Fashion subsumes the forefront of contemporary art. It always has, but in recent decades it seems to have loomed larger. From about 1860 to 1960 an avant-garde stood apart from the crowd. The salons and museums resisted it. Now the avant-garde *is* the crowd. Being "far-out" is in. I'm not suggesting that good art is no longer challenging, but that the *appearance* of challenge has become the current norm.

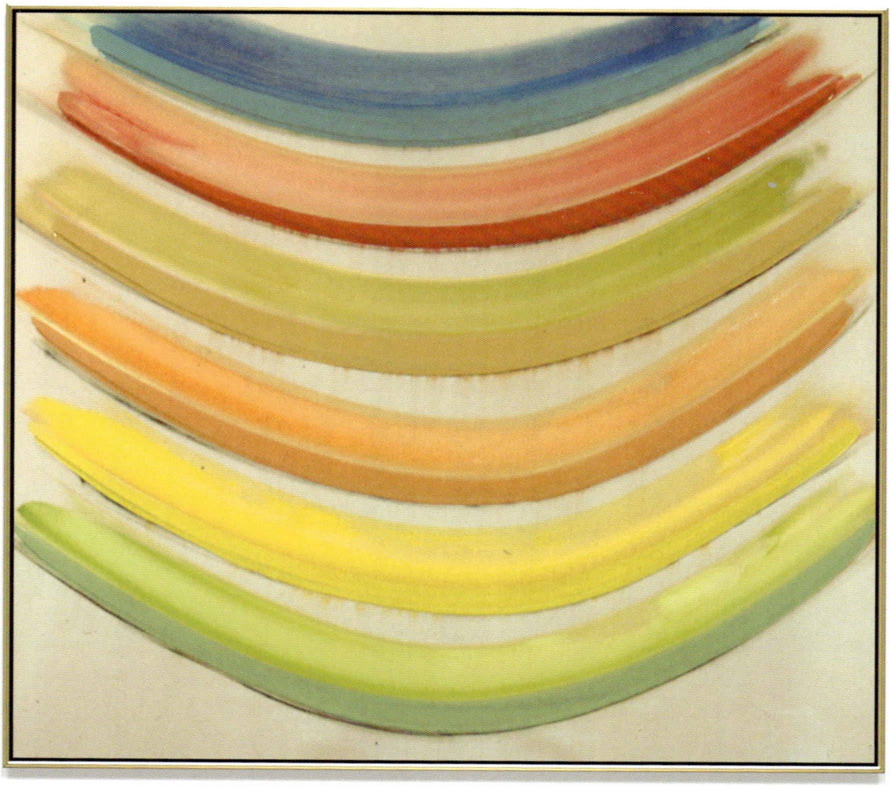

Robert Christie (Canadian 1946-), *Cambie Street Colour*, 1991.
Acrylic on canvas, 55½ x 64½ in. Mendel Art Gallery collection, gift of the artist.
Photograph © Mendel Art Gallery

This is a painting by a Canadian painter from Saskatoon. I'm reproducing it because I like it so much—it's one of the best paintings I acquired during the four years I was director of the Mendel Gallery in that city. The fact that the artist was local and Canadian was beside the point. Good pictures are good pictures, and this one is exceptional. If an abstract painting can be described as "happy", this one surely is. I added a frame and a bit of shadow to give a better idea of its presence on the wall. These days paintings are frequently exhibited sans frame, in many cases a mistake. They're almost always reproduced without frames, which may be a mistake as well.

It ain't necessarily so

Unfortunately many museums have mediocre works by great artists. This is to be expected; artists, collectors, and curators are seldom perfect. Most artistic failures are well meaning ones. Most collecting failures are self-deluded ones. Beware of received information. (If someone says, "everybody knows..." stop listening.) Be honest in your likes and dislikes, but don't be mean. Be wary of over-analysis, literary or formal.

ARTISTS

Genius

When I was 16, I was thrilled by Kirk Douglas's portrayal of Vincent Van Gogh in *Lust For Life*. Here, it seemed to me, was a speaking example of what it really meant to be an artist, and the gigantic, on-screen reproductions underscored it all. For several generations Van Gogh became the archetype of the tormented creative genius who died young. Jackson Pollock died in a motor accident (along with a frightened passenger) the year *Lust for Life* was released. *Pollock*, the movie, was released 46 years later in the year 2000. I haven't yet seen it, but I fear that it updated the myth of the tortured artist.

When it comes to artists we tend to substitute the adjective "tormented" for more accurate ones like "mentally ill," "alcoholic," or "self-destructive." The myths are misleading. Most artists aren't any more tormented than the general run of mankind. They raise families, pay taxes, and die of natural causes. Many support their art through unrelated employment.

In spite of this, a certain amount of torment seems to enhance reputations. Mark Rothko (1903-70), an important artist, died by his own hand. Adolph Gottlieb (1903-74), one of Rothko's contemporaries, didn't. Which was the better artist? I myself give the edge to Gottlieb. He painted more great pictures and his high accomplishment was more varied and went on longer than Rothko's. Some of his last works, done while confined to a wheel chair, were outstanding. To my eyes Rothko's art declined after the mid 1960s some years before his death.

Do yourself a favour: forget the myth of the tormented genius. Artists are human beings who make art. Some are tormented for one reason or another. Their work often declines as a result. Others aren't; their work sometimes declines as well. Judge the artist by his art.

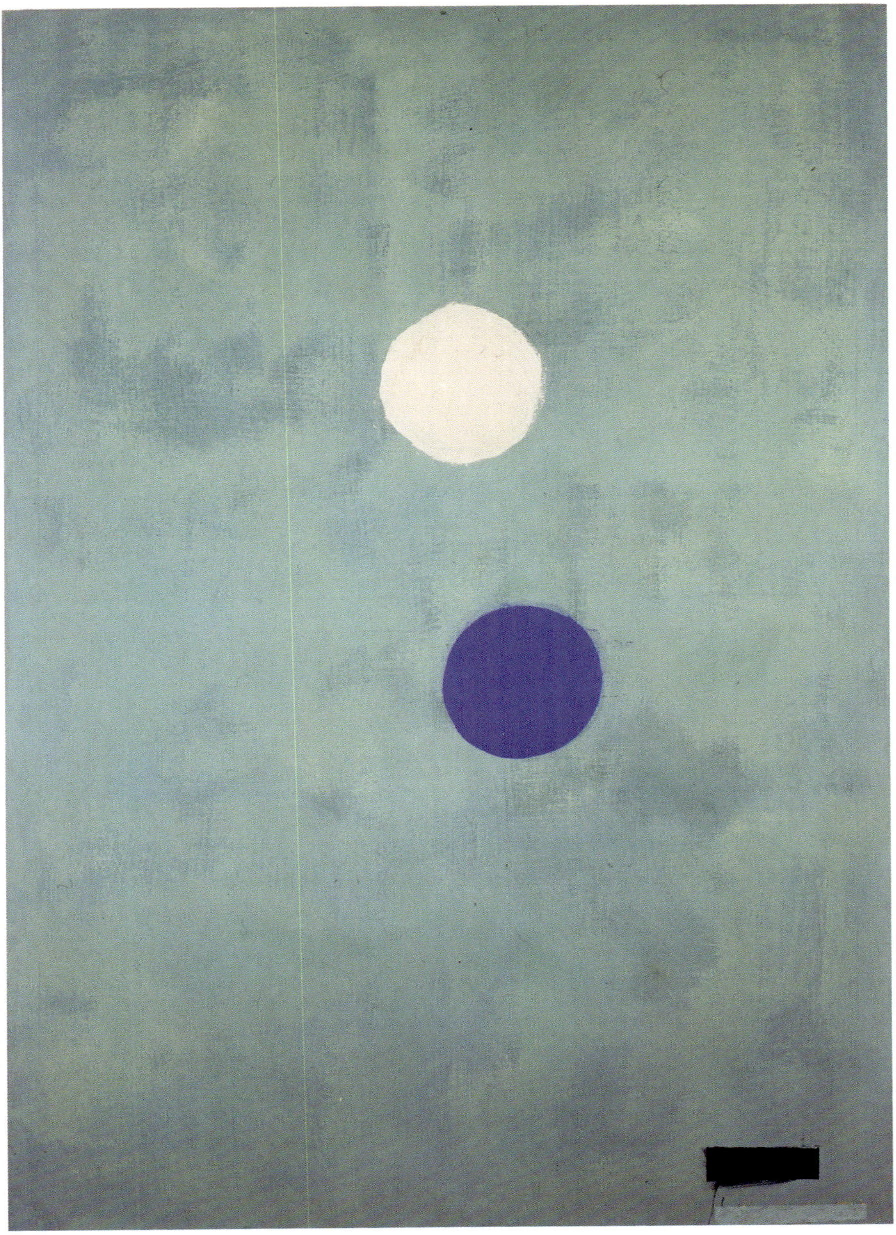

Adolph Gottlieb (American 1903-1974), *Blue Disc*, 1973. Acrylic on canvas, 84 x 60 in.
Photograph © Adolph and Esther Gottlieb Foundation / Licensed by VAGA, New York, NY

Gottlieb suffered a stroke in 1970, was paralyzed on his left side and continued to paint until his death in 1974, producing some of his finest and most adventurous works. This was painted during that period.

Jane Morris was the wife of William Morris, the great Victorian designer, poet, and socialist. Dante Gabriel Rossetti was an equally famous Pre Raphaelite poet and painter; Mrs. Morris was his favorite model. The photographer, John Parsons was presumably a friend of the Rossettis and Morrises. Rossetti's "genius" lost some of its lustre in the 20th Century, overshadowed by that of his poet sister, Christina. Presumably the photograph was posed with a Rossetti painting in mind. It's a wonderful picture, but who was the artist?

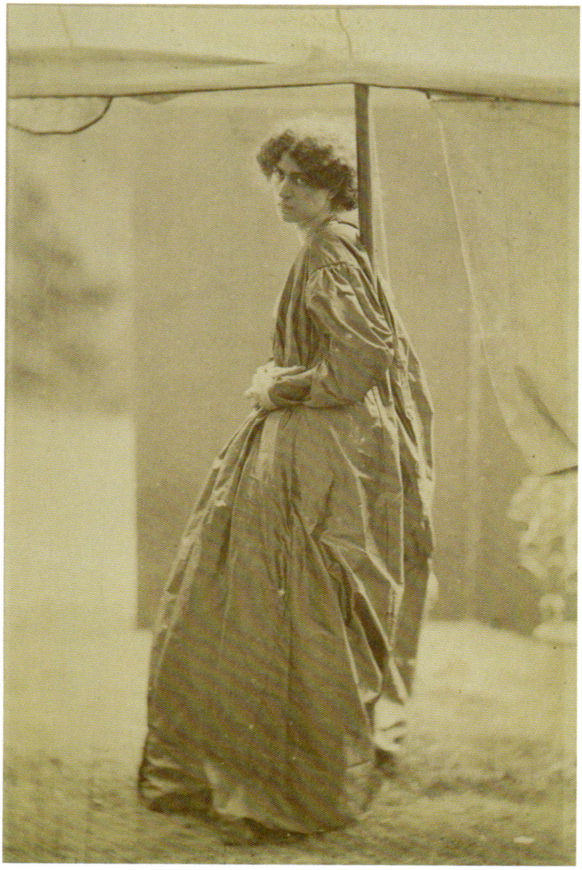

John R. Parsons (English), Jane Morris, posed by Rossetti, 1865.
Albumen print from wet collodion-on-glass negative, 7⅝ x 5⅛ in.
Victoria and Albert Museum
Photograph © Victoria and Albert Museum, London

Judgment

One of the hardest tasks faced by an artist is to judge his or her own art. For the artist, what is commonly called "creativity" consists in large part of the exercise of it.

Of necessity, art begins with some kind of conception. This isn't a simple thing; it involves choices of many things: medium, size, palette, subject, process, and a host of imponderables. Some of these can be changed during the making; others can't, at least not easily. Among these choices is a conception of the final product, sometimes little more than a glimmer. At times that glimmer can open a door, but it can also be an obstacle or a crutch. That's where judgment comes in: it must separate the actual from the ideal, the practice from the theory.

The better artist comes down on the side of what he sees as he works. He learns to value what his eyes tell him over and above his preconceptions and often his intentions. Sometimes those judgments are painful. If all artists were good at judging their own art we'd have more great artists. Alas, many falter somewhere along the way.

Creativity

How often have I been told that a work of art is the result of a "creative process?" The statement is generally a platitude. If artists are universally "creative" why is so much art mediocre? "Creativity" matters just as little as do artists' intentions and for much the same reason.

Its irrelevance is fundamental and begins with what I believe to be a basic fact about art, that what we call art is the art object in use: the *appreciated* art object. Apart from appreciation, art is just material, just "stuff." Appreciation, not creation, is the fundamental fact of art.

The concept of a creative process is an attempt to explain how art gets made. I'm not terribly interested in the attempt because it defies analysis and simply doesn't matter.

Is the appreciation of art restricted to human beings? Bird song comes immediately to mind as the art of another species. Bird song is often beautiful, but is it beautiful for the birds? And is it art in any but a rudimentary sense for us? It strikes me that it's a kind of pre-artistic phenomenon, the raw material or inspiration for art rather than art itself. But whatever it may be to us, the bird's "creativity" doesn't matter. Human appreciation of the song is what counts. To repeat: *appreciation* not *creation* is the central issue.

Nevertheless, the attempt to understand how art gets made is understandable. I say understandable because the categories of things which we refer to as art tend to be produced by human beings. We don't expect to find them occurring naturally (not withstanding the fact that we can appreciate aspects of nature). Because some individuals are particularly successful at making art we argue backward from the fact of the category, assuming some characteristic method of production. We suspect that some extraordinary psychology is involved, even a magical process like alchemy.

Certainly some psychological process attaches to the making of art, but who's to say that the process for artist (a) is the same as for artist (b)? Furthermore, it strikes me that these theories often assume that the nature of this psychological state is equivalent to the quality of the art it produces. No doubt it is sometimes, but that's not to say that it is always or necessarily.

So how does art get made? Most likely, I suspect, through a series of the artist's own appreciations interspersed with other kinds of activity: imagining, muddling around, doing nothing, working purposefully, working aimlessly. Some of this is undoubtedly conditioned by necessity and society and context, but not in any simple sense; above all not in any necessary sense. What I'm suggesting is that what we call "creativity" isn't necessarily one type of thing, and above all that making art is always governed by appreciation. The artist must have an internal audience; without it he can't make anything. But if he's wise, as Shakespeare almost certainly was, he'll test that audience against an external one, and if necessary make changes.

COLLECTING

Museums

Why visit museums?

To paraphrase Willie Sutton: because that's where they keep the pictures.

Art museums are—or once were—primarily picture galleries, thanks largely to the portability of the easel picture. They displayed "masterworks," mostly from the past. Many still do.

Large museums with extensive permanent collections are indispensable agents of culture. They assemble a lot of art in one place. They sort things out—usually by period and culture.

In the process, they tend to sanctify. They suggest—sometimes inadvertently—that art not found within their precincts doesn't quite measure up. When it comes to pictures, this obscures the fact that the great majority of them were made to decorate people's homes—and not always the homes of the very rich. Most paintings were made to be lived with. Most photographs were made to be leafed through. Museums are artificial environments—"social constructs," if you will. You can't live in them. You can't rearrange their contents on a whim; you can't glance at their contents over coffee.

Exhibitions

In the late 20th Century, when small and mid-sized public galleries began to proliferate, many lacked or couldn't afford "old masters." For this and a variety of other reasons, they mounted or hosted temporary exhibitions of contemporary art. These began to displace exhibitions drawn from what permanent collections they had: exhibitions brought new people in; changing exhibitions brought them back. In the 1960s and '70s most of these were exhibitions of pictures: solo exhibitions and group shows.

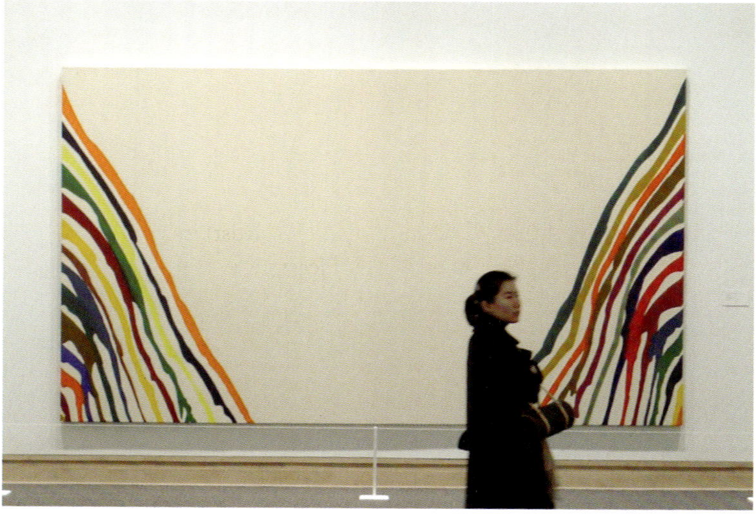

Morris Louis (American 1912-1962), *Alpha-Pi*, 1960. Metropolitan Museum of Art, Arthur Hoppock Hearn Fund, 1967.

One of Louis's great "Unfurleds," a big abstract painting. The museum visitor gives some idea of its size. Shown in situ at the Met. But why was it shown unframed?

In the 1980s and '90s exhibitions of pictures began to give way to exhibition installations in which pictures as pictures played a secondary role, if any. These "installations" tended to focus attention on a variety of social, political and cultural "issues;" the objects or images included were a means to a more "significant" end. But was the attention they focused aesthetic attention, or did they set aside the aesthetic in favour of something "higher?" The "significance" of subject matter tended to justify the enterprise. In my experience the aesthetic was generally impoverished.

In the 19th Century, romantic painting exalted subject matter over the more objective "rules" of neoclassical art. Modernism restored aesthetic objectivity, albeit in a new way. Today, post-modernism has swung the pendulum back to the significance of subjects. Will the picture as a work of art be a casualty of the change? Something like this seems to be taking place in the museums, where exhibitions and installations have begun to displace unique pictures and sculptures.

Pictures as decor

Despite my above observations, the art market remains an object market, and pictures of one kind or another retain a more prominent place there than they do in many of the museums. It's hard to sell installations. Moreover, most art buyers purchase pictures for their homes and businesses, for decor.

In the 1960s a museum director I knew (and more than one artist) insisted that Henri Matisse was "just a decorator." They maintained that Picasso was the more significant artist. Though they didn't say so, I suspect they thought that Picasso's paintings of the 1930s and '40s—"Guernica" among them—grappled with "issues" while Matisse peacefully painted nudes and interiors in the south of France. Today Picasso's later work seems a kind of accomplished illustration while Matisse is more highly regarded now than he was in his lifetime. What was once dismissed as décor (which Matisse's paintings supremely were) seems richer and more life affirming than most latter-day Picassos.

Why collect?

Why bother to collect art? Why have so many people done it for so many centuries? By art I mean art in its largest sense: manuscripts and documents; costumes, rugs, pottery, and other decorative objects; paintings and sculpture: the wonderful, material things we stick in museums from all of human history. Why have they been saved? Who saved them?

Time tends to destroy. The natural enemies of art are slow decomposition and sudden destruction. The human ones are even worse: war, indifference, and vandalism. The combination is replete with irony. Early in the 20th Century, priceless Chinese manuscripts were unearthed in the Gobi desert where they'd lain hidden for over 2,000 years. Many went to a Berlin museum where they were destroyed by Allied bombing during WWII. On the other hand, in the 19th Century Lord Elgin removed sculptures from the Parthenon in Greece. If he hadn't they'd have been salvaged by the Turks for limestone, or lost piecemeal to souvenir hunters. Today they're in the British Museum and the Greek Government wants them back. Meanwhile, the Parthenon is crumbling away because of air pollution in Athens. Was Lord Elgin a destroyer or preserver? The jury's still out.

Fortunately, humans aren't always destructive. The collections in our finest museums attest to that. Their great pictures weren't painted for museums but primarily for individuals. Individuals preserved and protected them by living with them.

So, if YOU want to buy art

Do find out what you, yourself, like. You'll have a better chance of buying good art if you do. But to do so, you must learn to trust your eyes. **Don't** assume that that's an easy task.

Don't expect consistency from good artists. Good artists are often inconsistent. Uniform quality is often uniform mediocrity.

Don't be afraid to focus on an artist or a period or a medium. But let that decision come with experience.

Don't be afraid of making mistakes. Learn from them. When you do that, mistakes become your friends.

Do visit museums and dealers when you travel. Don't purchase art when on vacation, especially in resort destinations; you're liable to pay more for less or acquire "tourist art."

Do look for a friend to share at least some of your interests.

Do learn whose eyes you can trust (not necessarily someone from the art world).

Contemporary art

Are pictures worth buying today? Certainly pictures from that past are, as auction records insist. But what about contemporary art?

Until World War II, the best contemporary art was made in Paris; after that in New York. (This wasn't just a matter of fashion, though fashion clouded the issue.) Not quite so today. Despite the fact that New York remains the great marketplace for contemporary art, fewer and fewer ambitious artists live there and trendiness has flourished elsewhere, most recently in London. There are two reasons for this: in recent years it has become increasingly difficult for young foreign artists to live and work in the United States, and the city has become so expensive that few young artists can afford to live there (recently they've made inroads into Brooklyn). Still, if one is to collect contemporary art seriously, one must pay attention to New York as to no other city.

Collecting contemporary art is challenging. It often involves buying apart from the security of a strong secondary market and in an environment in which rumor and hearsay flourish. A lot of big-name contemporary art is mediocre at best. Remember that the best art of the past century and a half was seldom highly regarded when it was new.

Nothing has changed.

But if collected well, the quality to price ratio of contemporary art is extremely high and the adventure of discovery is its own reward.

But I'd still like to own that Bellini.

Notes

1 Oliver Sacks, "In the River of Consciousness", *New York Review of Books*, Volume 51, Number 1 - January 15, 2004

2 Henri Matisse, "Notes of a Painter 1908", *Matisse on Art*, Jack D. Flan, ed., Oxford, 1973.

3 John Ruskin, "Michelangelo and Tintoret", *The Lamp of Beauty, Writings on Art by John Ruskin*, Selected and edited by Joan Evans. London, 1959, p. 120.

4 Heinrich Wölfflin, *Principles of Art History*, New York, 1950, p. 30.

5 "Walter Pater, "The School of Giorgione," *The Renaissance.*

6 Henri Matisse, Op. cit, "Notes of a Painter."

Recommended Reading & Viewing

Books

Berenson, Bernard, *Aesthetics and History*

Berenson, Bernard, *Italian Painters of the Renaissance*

Clark, Kenneth, *Landscape Into Art*

Delacroix, Eugene, *Journals*

Freedberg, Sydney J., *Painting in Italy, 1500-1600*

Friedländer, Max J., *Landscape, Portrait, Still Life*

Fry, Roger, *Art And Design*

Fry, Roger, *Giovanni Bellini*

Greenberg, Clement, *The collected Essays and Criticism, Vols. 1-4*

Greenberg, Clement, *Late Writings*

Hauser, Arnold, *The Social History of Art*

Pater, Walter, "The School of Giorgione", *The Renaissance*

Pevsner, Nikolaus, *The Englishness of English Art*

Reynolds, Sir Joshua, *Discourses on Art*

Ruskin, John, *Modern Painters Vols. I-V*

Vasari, Giorgio, *Lives of the Painters, Sculptors, and Architects*

Wölfflin, Heinrich, *Principles of Art History*

Web Sites

Artcyclopedia: www.artcyclopedia.com/

British Museum Images: www.bmimages.com/

Cleveland Museum of Art: www.clemusart.com/explore/

Frick Collection, New York: www.frick.org/collection/index.htm

Hirshhorn Museum and Sculpture Garden: hirshhorn.si.edu/search.asp

J. Paul Getty Museum: www.getty.edu/art/gettyguide/

Metropolitan Museum, New York:
www.metmuseum.org/works_of_art/collection_database/

Museum of Fine Arts, Boston www.mfa.org/collections/

Museum of Modern Art (MoMA): www.moma.org/collection/

National Gallery, London: www.nationalgalleryimages.co.uk/

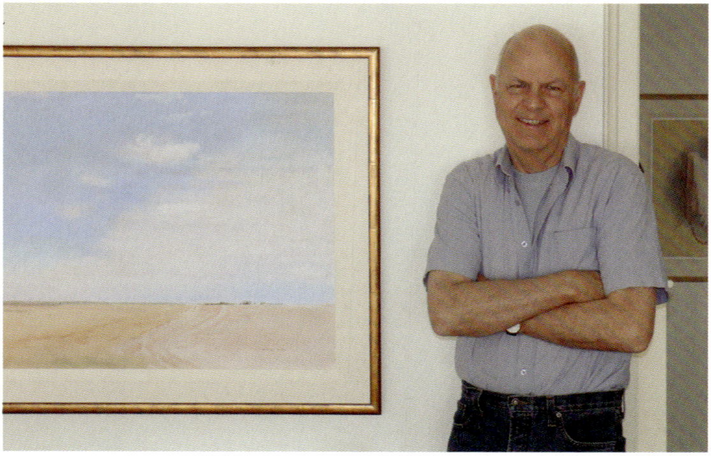

Photo by Sheila Fenton

Biography

Terry Fenton is a well known curator, museum director, writer, and artist. Although based in the Canadian West, his achievements have brought international recognition.

From 1972-1988 Fenton was Director of The Edmonton Art Gallery, where he helped to make Edmonton a centre for both the collection and creation of art. As Director of the Leighton Foundation in Calgary, 1988-1993, he developed programs for landscape painters. From 1993-1997, he was Director of the Mendel Art Gallery in Saskatoon where he continues to live while writing extensively on art and painting in his studio in the historic York building.

Fenton's publications include:

Modern Painting in Canada (co-written with Karen Wilkin), 1978

Anthony Caro, 1986

Appreciating Noland, 1990

Reta Summers Cowley, 2007

Land Marks, The Art of Dorothy Knowles, 2008

Fenton's website:

www.sharecom.ca/fenton/